◆ THE FILMS OF ◆
MARILYN MONROE

by Richard Buskin

Publications International, Ltd.

Photo credits:

Cinema Collectors: Front cover, 3, 4, 5, 6, 7, 8, 10, 11 (bottom right & bottom), 12 (bottom), 13, 14, 16 (top), 17, 18 (bottom), 19 (top & bottom right), 20 (bottom), 21 (top), 22, 23, 24, 26, 27 (bottom right), 28, 29 (bottom left & bottom right), 30 (bottom), 31, 33 (top), 34 (bottom), 35 (top right), 36 (bottom), 37 (top), 39, 40 (bottom), 41 (top), 42, 43, 44, 45 (top left & bottom), 46 (bottom), 47, 50, 51, 52, 53, 54, 55 (top), 56 (center & bottom), 57 (top left & top right), 58, 59, 60 (bottom left & bottom right), 61 (top left & bottom), 62 (top), 63 (bottom), 64 (bottom), 65, 66, 68 (bottom left & bottom right), 69, 70, 71 (bottom), 72, 73 (top left & bottom), 74, 75 (top), 76 (top & center), 77, 78, 79 (bottom), 80, 81 (top left & bottom), 82, 83 (bottom), 84, 86, 87 (bottom), 88, 89, 91 (bottom), 92, 93, 94 (top), 95, 96 (bottom); **Globe Photos, Inc.**/L. Schiller: 90, 94 (center & bottom); **Tom Jacobs Collection:** 29 (top), 41 (bottom); **Ron Jung Collection:** 55 (bottom), 56 (top), 57 (bottom), 62 (bottom), 63 (top), 67 (top & bottom), 68 (top & center), 71 (top) ©1955 William Inge Bantam Books, 75 (bottom), 76 (bottom), 79 (top), 83 (top) ©1960 United Newspapers Magazine Corporation, 85 (left), 87 (top) ©1961 Cowles Magazines & Broadcasting, Inc., 91 (top), 96 (top); **Movie Still Archives:** 9 (top), 16 (bottom), 19 (bottom), 25 (top left & bottom), 27 (top & bottom left), 35 (bottom), 36 (top), 37 (bottom), 49 (bottom); **Jerry Ohlinger's, Inc.:** 12 (top), 15 (top & bottom), 18 (top), 20 (top), 30 (top), 38, 40 (top), 46 (top), 48 (top), 60 (top), 64 (top); **Photofest:** 9 (bottom), 11 (top), 21 (bottom), 25 (top right), 32, 33 (bottom), 35 (top left), 45 (top right), 48 (bottom), 49 (top), 61 (top right), 73 (top right), 81 (top right), 85 (right).

Richard Buskin is a freelance film and music journalist based in London, England. His interviews, feature stories, and photographs have been published in a variety of magazines all over the world. Buskin previously chronicled John Lennon's life and career in *John Lennon: His Life and Legend*.

The author would like to thank the following for their assistance in unearthing new details in regard to Marilyn Monroe:

Henry Schipper, producer, writer, and narrator of *Marilyn: Something's Got to Give*
Shawn Griggs and Vanessa Reyes, Fox Broadcasting Company
Patrick Miller, Twentieth Century-Fox Library
David Shepherd, University of Southern California
Arlene Donovan, ICM in New York
Walter Bernstein, screenwriter for *Something's Got to Give*
Bob Iuliucci and Allen J. Wiener, research
And, the Staff of the invaluable British Film Institute Library

LADIES OF THE CHORUS

NIAGARA

RIVER OF NO RETURN

CONTENTS

BUS STOP

SOME LIKE IT HOT

THE MISFITS

FADE-IN

Marilyn Monroe: Legendary in her own lifetime, enigmatic in death.

Was Marilyn Monroe a great actress?

Opinions vary as to the acting talents of this enigmatic, child-like woman with the breathy voice and hourglass figure. Whatever her talents, Marilyn's on-screen image and offscreen lifestyle captured the public imagination during her lifetime and continue to do so nearly three decades after her death.

Beautiful, sensual, vulnerable, affable . . . MM was all of these, and much more. A heady mixture of glamour, lust, and fun, she was able to flaunt her charms while always maintaining her dignity, gaining her not only the undivided attention of men but also the sympathy and admiration of women. Acting skill aside, Marilyn Monroe was—and is—the archetypal screen goddess.

Between 1948 and 1961 she appeared in 29 films, bringing to each a luminous quality that has rarely been matched. More than just turning on the sex appeal when required, Marilyn excelled at making love to the principal ally of her career—the camera.

Having served her apprenticeship by appearing on the covers of numerous magazines during the mid- to late-1940s, Marilyn (then Norma Jeane Dougherty) came to Hollywood with a comprehensive knowledge of how to best project her vital statistics. In part, this was due to her tremendous dedication to her profession, tirelessly studying the points that needed perfecting and ever-willing to listen to the advice of others. When Emmeline Snively of the Blue Book Model Agency informed her, "There isn't enough upper lip between the end of your nose and your mouth," Norma Jeane responded by learning to lower her lip when she smiled. With practice, and the addition of a slight quiver, this later became an MM trademark.

The other major factor contributing to her appeal in front of the lens was something that simply cannot be taught. In short, she was a complete natural. Photographers and cameramen who had worked with Marilyn have attested to the way in which her sometimes ordinary appearance inevitably transformed itself into extraordinary results on film. "When she saw a camera, any camera, she lit up and was totally different," confirmed Laszlo Willinger, who photographed her during the 1940s. "Then, the moment the shot was over, she fell back into her not-very-interesting position, and I don't know how to explain that."

Leon Shamroy was the cinematographer on Marilyn's 1946 screen test, just prior to gaining her first contract with Twentieth Century-Fox. The veteran cameraman remembered getting "a cold chill" while watching the screening of the color test, which featured Marilyn walking across the set in a sequined gown, sitting down, lighting a cigarette, looking out a window, and then walking off. "This girl had something I hadn't seen since silent pictures," Shamroy claimed. "She had a kind of fantastic beauty like Gloria Swanson, when a movie star had to look beautiful, and she got sex on a piece of film like Jean Harlow."

1940s-vintage Norma Jeane Dougherty, showing off the figure that would launch her on the road to immortality.

THE FILMS OF MARILYN MONROE

Lawrence Schiller photographed the 36-year-old star on the set of her last film, the never-completed *Something's Got to Give*. He recalled, "She came out of the dressing room Norma Jeane. When she stepped in front of the camera, she was Marilyn."

The testimonies of these photographers and cameramen confirm that Marilyn Monroe was a first-rate model, but they do not fully answer the question regarding her abilities as an actress. Acting was a craft that she made great strides to understand and to master, and, though in the end such efforts did not help her overcome her personal problems, they greatly enhanced her performances. "I knew how third-rate I was," Marilyn once said, looking back on her early years as a movie starlet. "I could actually feel my lack of talent, as if it were cheap clothes I was wearing inside. But, my God, how I wanted to learn! To change, to improve. I didn't want anything else. Not men, not money, not love, but the ability to act!"

Her first move in this direction was to take instruction from Phoebe Brand as well as Morris Carnovsky at the Actors Lab in Hollywood, but it wasn't until Columbia's head drama coach, Natasha Lytess, quit her job and took her under her wing that Marilyn really began to improve as an actress.

Lytess, a former student of German drama director Max Reinhardt, looked beyond the image of the dumb blonde bombshell and discovered an intelligent, inquiring mind, and she resolved to bring this out on the screen. She set about developing the talent that lay just beneath the surface, and within a few years she helped transform Marilyn from the characterless ingenue of *Ladies of the Chorus* (1948) into a performer of considerable depth in *Don't Bother to Knock* (1952) and *Niagara* (1953), as well as an adroit comedienne in *Gentlemen Prefer Blondes* (1953), *How to Marry a Millionaire* (1953), and, most notably, *The Seven Year Itch* (1955).

At the end of 1954, Marilyn decided that a steady stream of formularized, "sexy blonde" vehicles was not helping to achieve her ambition of becoming a serious actress. She then undertook the extremely brave step of leaving Hollywood for New York, forming her own production company, and enrolling in classes at the famed Actors Studio.

Left: *Lighting up in front of the camera, to produce what Cecil Beaton described as "the bouquet of fireworks display."* Right: *Drama coach Natasha Lytess with her young protégée, c. 1948.*

During the 1950s, the Actors Studio was at the height of its acclaim, having gained both notoriety and respect for its teaching of the then-controversial Method style of acting. The Method, which derived from the teachings of Konstantin Stanislavski, required performers to draw on personal experiences and look inside a character before fully immersing themselves in a role; a case of quite literally becoming somebody else, rather than simply learning lines and playing a part.

Lee Strasberg presided over the Studio, and during the 1950s, his pupils included Montgomery Clift, Marlon Brando, James Dean, Paul Newman, and Rod Steiger, yet he once stated that Brando and Marilyn Monroe were the greatest acting talents he had ever coached. Marilyn proved worthy of Strasberg's praise when, on her return to Hollywood in 1956, she gave an outstanding performance in the comic drama *Bus Stop*. "Monroe is as near genius as any actress I ever knew," the director of *Bus Stop*, Joshua Logan, later recalled. "Watch her work. In any film. How rarely she has to use words. How much she does with her eyes, her lips, with slight, almost accidental gestures . . . Monroe is pure cinema."

Reinforced by a ground-breaking new contract with Fox, which gave her approval not only over the story-lines of her films but also over the director and cinematographer, and aided by daily coaching from Strasberg's wife, Paula, Marilyn proceeded to confound the critics who had tried to categorize her as just another sex symbol. Thereafter, Marilyn was not just a movie star in the eyes of critics and moviegoers, she *was* Elsie Marina in *The Prince and the Showgirl* (1957), Sugar Kane in *Some Like It Hot* (1959), and Roslyn Taber in her last completed film, *The Misfits* (1961). She also performed admirably in the company of such accomplished actors as Laurence Olivier, Jack Lemmon, Clark Gable, and fellow Actors Studio classmate Eli Wallach.

In the final analysis, Marilyn Monroe had many on-screen virtues: She had warmth, charm, pathos, a good sense of timing, great looks, undeniable charisma, and a style that has been often imitated but never duplicated. Whether all of this indicated that she was a really great actress is still open to debate, but what is beyond doubt is that she was a truly great star . . . a male fantasy . . . a female phenomenon . . . the stuff that legends are made of.

Left: *Displaying the attribute that prompted Constance Bennett to describe her as "a broad with her future behind her."* Right: *Black-clad Paula Strasberg, MM's last coach, surveys production.*

THE FILMS OF MARILYN MONROE

SCUDDA HOO! SCUDDA HAY!

Striving to look like Betty Grable, the Queen of the Fox lot.

Farm hand Snug Dominy contracts to buy a pair of mules from his employer, Roarer McGill. The problem with the animals is that no one is able to handle them, but Snug is determined to keep the contract so he makes great efforts to overcome their stubbornness. In the meantime, he also has to contend with the antics of the boss's daughter, Rad, who is in love with Snug but enjoys whiling away her time keeping him guessing about her true feelings. In the end, of course, Snug gets both the mules and the girl.

BEHIND THE SCENES

Scudda Hoo! Scudda Hay! has the distinction of being the first Hollywood film that Marilyn Monroe ever appeared in, but this offbeat comedy hardly makes the most of her presence. Cast in a bit part as a farm girl, she had a one-line speaking role—either "Hi, Rad" or "Hello"—but, according to most sources, the line was subsequently edited out. Marilyn herself believed that her one line had been cut and repeated this information in a 1955 television interview. Disputing this commonly held notion is noted Monroe expert James Haspiel, who maintains that in complete versions of the film, her line is intact. This discrepancy aside, Monroe authorities agree she appears in a scene at a lake, where people can be seen relaxing and swimming. In the background two girls are rowing in a canoe. Their faces are not clearly visible, but, rest assured, one of them is Marilyn!

Wisely retitled *Summer Lightning* in certain markets, the movie—which also features a nine-year-old Natalie Wood—was made in early 1947, during the initial six-month option of Marilyn's contract with Twentieth Century-Fox. Its release, however, followed that of the second film that she appeared in, *Dangerous Years*.

With only a short-term contract from Fox, MM had to keep up her modeling career.

CAST

Rad McGill . . . . .June Haver
Snug Dominy . .Lon McCallister
Tony Maule . . .Walter Brennan
Judith Dominy . . .Anne Revere
Bean McGill. . . .Natalie Wood
Stretch Dominy . .Robert Karnes
Milt Dominy . . . .Henry Hull
Roarer McGill . . . .Tom Tully
Ches . . . . . .Les MacGregor
Mrs. McGill . . .Geraldine Wall
Sheriff Bursom . . .Ken Christy
Judge Stillwell . . . .Tom Moore
Jim . . . . . . .Matt McHugh
Barber . . .Charles Wagenheim
Dugan . . . .Herbert Heywood
Ted . . . . . .Edward Gargan
Elmer. . . . . . . .Guy Beach
Malone. . . . . .G. Pat Collins
Jeff . . . . . .Charles Woolf
Stable Hand . . .Eugene Jackson
Girl Friends . .Colleen Townsend,
Marilyn Monroe

CREDITS

Twentieth Century-Fox

Produced by Walter Morosco

Directed and written by
F. Hugh Herbert

Based on a story by
George Agnew Chamberlain

Photographed in Technicolor by
Ernest Palmer

Art direction by Lyle Wheeler and
Albert Hogsett

Music by Cyril Mockridge

Music conducted by
Lionel Newman

Released April 1948

Top: *Colleen Townsend and Marilyn Monroe's scenes with Robert Karnes ended up on the cutting-room floor.* Bottom: *But established stars June Haver and Natalie Wood were more fortunate.*

THE FILMS OF MARILYN MONROE

DANGEROUS YEARS

Successfully proving her theory that "cheesecake helps call attention to you."

The new contract player poses for the publicity department on the Fox lot, c. 1947.

School teacher Jeff Carter spends his spare time running a social club for teenage boys. His efforts are undermined by the arrival of Danny Jones, a flashy troublemaker who involves others, including Doris, Willy, and Leo, in petty criminal activities. Things come to a head when Leo informs Jeff about a planned raid on a warehouse. Carter intercepts the robbery, but in the process he is shot and killed by Danny. At the trial, it is revealed that Danny was raised in the same orphanage as Connie, the daughter of District Attorney Edgar Burns. She was born after her parents' separation, and Burns only learned of her existence when contacted by a nurse at the orphanage. What is not known, however, is that the nurse was lying. She felt sorry for Connie, who was sick, and hoped that Burns would provide her with better surroundings. In truth, the D.A.'s child is Danny! The nurse informs Danny of this, but, convicted and sentenced to jail, he decides to keep the secret to himself.

BEHIND THE SCENES

Dangerous Years, an obscure "B" movie, was typical of the fare produced by Sol M. Wurtzel, who had entered the Hollywood industry back in 1914 when he joined a production company owned by William Fox. Fox's company eventually evolved into Twentieth Century-Fox, with Wurtzel outlasting Fox himself in the film business. Over the years, Wurtzel became known for turning out a string of minor, low-budget pictures, prompting the quip that Fox's product was "going from bad to Wurtzel!" In spite of this, Marilyn's role as Evie, the waitress at a jukebox joint, provided her with her first on-screen lines. She responds to a fresh-faced kid's greeting of "Hi, Evie," with an offhanded, "Hi, small change!"

For their part, the powers that be at Fox were not overly impressed with Marilyn and dropped her contract. Forced to live in a succession of furnished rooms while trying to continue with her lessons at the Actors Lab, Marilyn turned to modeling once again in order to pay her own bills.

CAST

Danny Jones . . .William Halop
Doris Martin . . . .Ann E. Todd
Weston . . . . . .Jerome Cowan
Connie Burns . . .Anabel Shaw
Edgar Burns . . .Richard Gaines
Willy Miller . . .Scotty Beckett
Leo Emerson . .Darryl Hickman
Judge Raymond . .Harry Shannon
Gene Spooner . . .Dickie Moore
Jeff Carter . . . .Donald Curtis
Phil Kenny . . .Harry Harvey, Jr.
Tammy McDonald . . . . . .
. . . . .Gil Stratton, Jr.
August Miller . . .Joseph Vitale
Evie . . . . . .Marilyn Monroe
Miss Templeton . . .Nana Bryant

CREDITS

Twentieth Century-Fox

Produced by Sol M. Wurtzel

Directed by Arthur Pierson

Story and screenplay by
Arnold Belgard

Photographed by Benjamin Kline

Art direction by Walter Koessler

Music by Rudy Schrager

Released February 1948

Modeling became Marilyn's chief means of support when Fox dropped her contract.

Top: *"Look, this tray weighs a ton," grumbles Evie to a young punk who is trying to date her.*
Bottom: *Yet, she clearly has time to spare for the handsome older man.*

THE FILMS OF MARILYN MONROE

LADIES OF THE CHORUS

MM's contract with Columbia Pictures was dropped before this backstage drama was released.

Just before filming, MM's slightly protruding front teeth had been surgically corrected.

Mother and daughter, May and Peggy Martin, dance together in the chorus line of a burlesque show that May once starred in. When the current headliner, Bubbles LaRue, quits the show after a row with May, Peggy steps into her shoes. She becomes an instant hit and attracts the attentions of wealthy, young Randy Carroll. May fears that Randy's mother will break Peggy's heart by disapproving of the mismatch once she discovers the girl's profession. May urges her prospective son-in-law to tell his mother the truth before she throws an engagement party for the two love-birds, but he loses his nerve. As things turn out, they need not have worried. When a bandleader at the party recognizes Peggy and reveals a part of her background, Mrs. Carroll demonstrates her belief that love is more important than social status. Quelling potential gossip among the guests, she invents a glorious past in show business for Peggy and gives the young couple her blessing. Happy and relieved, May in turn celebrates by deciding to wed her own longtime boyfriend, comedian Billy Mackay.

B E H I N D   T H E   S C E N E S

Having signed Marilyn to a contract for $125 a week on March 9, 1948, Columbia Pictures placed her in this "B" musical, which was filmed in just 11 days. *Ladies of the Chorus* gave MM her first costarring role and the opportunity to sing on-screen for the first time. Assisting her were the studio's acting and vocal coaches, Natasha Lytess and Fred Karger, both of whom played important parts in MM's career. It was Karger who arranged to have Marilyn's slightly protruding front teeth fixed and who introduced her to classical music, fine literature, and the Hollywood social scene.

The results of such efforts were not immediately evident in *Ladies of the Chorus*, even though MM's immature yet charming performance prompted Tibor Krekes, the reviewer for *Motion Picture Herald*, to comment, "One of the bright spots is Miss Monroe's singing. She is pretty and, with her pleasing voice and style, she shows promise."

CAST

May Martin . . .	.Adele Jergens
Peggy Martin .	.Marilyn Monroe
Randy Carroll . .	.Rand Brooks
Mrs. Carroll . . .	.Nana Bryant
Billy Mackay . . .	.Eddie Garr
Salisbury	.Steven Geray
Alan Wakefield . .	.Bill Edwards
Bubbles LaRue . .	. . . . .
. . . . . .	.Marjorie Hoshelle
Joe	.Frank Scannell
Ripple	.Dave Barry
Ripple, Jr.. . . .	.Myron Healey
Peter Winthrop .	.Robert Clarke
Flower Shop Girl .	.Gladys Blake
Doctor.	.Emmett Vogan

CREDITS

Columbia Pictures

Produced by Harry A. Romm

Directed by Phil Karlson

Screenplay by Harry Sauber and
Joseph Carol

From a story by Harry Sauber

Photographed by Frank Redma

Art direction by Robert Peterson

Musical direction by
Mischa Bakaleinikoff

Production numbers staged by
Jack Boyle

Released February 1949

SONGS BY MM

"Every Baby Needs a
Da Da Daddy"

"Anyone Can Tell I Love You"

Top: *Former beauty queen Adele Jergens portrays Marilyn's mother in the film.* Bottom: *Yet, there was less than nine years age difference between the two women.*

THE FILMS OF MARILYN MONROE

LOVE HAPPY

Ilona Massey was "Screendom's most beautiful blonde," yet Marilyn held greater promotional value.

The struggling Love Happy *starlet, a month after posing for the infamous nude calender shots.*

STORYLINE

Detective Sam Grunion recounts the story of the missing Romanoff diamonds: Smuggled into the U.S. in a sardine can by Madame Egilichi and her colleagues, the diamonds end up in the hands of Harpo, who craftily purloins food for a struggling acting troupe. Tracing the missing loot to the theater where the actors are staging a musical, Egilichi's vain hopes of subtly retrieving the elusive can are dashed when Harpo discovers its contents on the opening night of the show. The ensuing chase around the roof of the building between the gun-toting band of smugglers and the diamond-toting petty thief comes to an abrupt end when Detective Grunion arrives on the scene. The detective's bumbling attempts to solve the case pave the way for Harpo's escape and—as Grunion informs us at the end of his tale—for his own marriage . . . to Madame Egilichi!

BEHIND THE SCENES

Though this was Marilyn's fourth film, and she was hired for only a brief walk-on part, the opening credits for *Love Happy* announced that it was "Introducing Marilyn Monroe." Marilyn may have appeared in films before, but *Love Happy* did introduce something special—the famous MM walk. Marilyn was informed by Groucho Marx that the role called for "a young lady who can walk by me in such a manner as to arouse my elderly libido and cause smoke to issue from my ears." Marilyn duly obliged, and she was promptly cast.

Broke and out of work, Marilyn accepted producer Lester Cowan's offer to tour the country promoting *Love Happy*. Dubbed by publicity men as "The Woo Woo Girl" and "The Mmmm Girl," she arrived for the first time in New York City and made some key connections. After moving on to Detroit, Cleveland, Chicago, Milwaukee, and Rockford, Illinois, Marilyn decided that she had enough of the promotional merry-go-round. She returned to Hollywood in August over the protests of Cowan.

CAST

Harpo . . . . . . .Harpo Marx
Faustino the Great . . . . . .
. . . . .Chico Marx
Sam Grunion . . .Groucho Marx
Madame Egilichi . .Ilona Massey
Maggie Phillips . . . .Vera-Ellen
Bunny Dolan . . .Marion Hutton
Mike Johnson . . .Paul Valentine
Alphonse Zoto . .Raymond Burr
Hannibal Zoto . .Bruce Gordon
Throckmorton . .Melville Cooper
Makinaw. . . . . . .Eric Blore
Mr. Lyons . . . . .Leon Belasco
Grunion's Client . . . .
. . . . . . .Marilyn Monroe

CREDITS

A United Artists release of a
Mary Pickford Presentation

Produced by Lester Cowan

Directed by David Miller

Screenplay by Frank Tashlin and
Mac Benoff

Based on a story by Harpo Marx

Photographed by
William C. Mellor

Art direction by
Gabriel Scognamillo

Music score by Ann Bonell

Released March 1950

Top: *There's no doubting what is on Sam Grunion's mind when a pretty blonde asks for his help.*
Bottom: *"I have a little sand left; what seems to be the trouble?" he inquires.*

THE FILMS OF MARILYN MONROE

A TICKET TO TOMAHAWK

A wardrobe test for a 19th-century costume, which is slightly less revealing than some of MM's other screen outfits.

A spot of hoofing with Dan Dailey.

STORYLINE

Dawson, the crooked owner of a stagecoach line, decides to eradicate his competition by sabotaging the journey of Engine One, the *Emma Sweeney*, of the Tomahawk and Western Railroad. If the engine is late in arriving at Tomahawk, Colorado, its owners will lose their trading license. Dawson hires a gunman named Dakota to cause a delay. The engine comes to a halt when it is discovered that there are no rails between Epitaph and Dead Horse Point. Kit, the granddaughter of U.S. Marshal Dodge, steps in with a team of mules to help drag the train toward other tracks. She requisitions the services of Johnny Behind-the-Deuces to accompany the vehicle and its passengers on the trip through dangerous Indian terrain. Johnny solves the dilemma by making a pact with the Indian tribe, and the train reaches its destination on time in spite of Dakota and Dawson. The Tomahawk and Western Railroad company retains its charter, and Johnny decides that his future lay in a life with Kit.

BEHIND THE SCENES

Marilyn's bit part in *A Ticket to Tomahawk* brought her back to the Twentieth Century-Fox lot for the first time since the studio had dropped her on August 25, 1947. Still a freelance actress, she was hired to sing, dance, and look pretty by casting director and former actor Ben Lyon. Lyon had arranged for her first screen test back in 1946 and had given her her stage name in the process.

After months of struggling, things were about to change for Marilyn. Superagent Johnny Hyde, a 53-year-old vice president of the William Morris Agency, had seen an advance screening of *Love Happy*, and he had noticed Marilyn. At a party in Palm Springs in 1949 he came face to face with her and fell madly in love. In spite of a heart condition, Hyde worked tirelessly to bring his influence to bear on the moguls who could help her. By the time *A Ticket to Tomahawk* was released in the spring of 1950, Marilyn had garnered a small but significant role in *The Asphalt Jungle*.

CAST

Johnny Behind-the-Deuces. . . .
. . . . .Dan Dailey
Kit Dodge, Jr. . . .Anne Baxter
Dakota . . . . . .Rory Calhoun
Terence Sweeny . .Walter Brennan
Chuckity . . . .Charles Kemper
Madame Adelaide . . . .
. . . . . . .Connie Gilchrist
Sad Eyes . . .Arthur Hunnicutt
Dodge . . . . . . .Will Wright
Pawnee . . . . .Chief Yowlachie
Dawson . . . . .Mauritz Hugo
Crooked Knife . . . .
. . . . . .Chief Thundercloud
Long Time . . .Victor Sen Yung
Mayor . . . .Raymond Greenleaf
Charley . . . . . .Harry Carter
Velvet Fingers . .Harry Seymour
Annie . . . . .Marion Marshall
Ruby . . . . .Joyce McKenzie
Clara. . . . .Marilyn Monroe
Julie. . . . . .Barbara Smith
Fargo . . . . . . .Jack Elam

CREDITS

Twentieth Century-Fox

Produced by Robert Bassler

Directed by Richard Sale

Screenplay by Mary Loos and
Richard Sale

Photographed in Technicolor by
Harry Jackson

Art direction by Lyle Wheeler and
George W. Davis

Music by Cyril Mockridge

Released May 1950

MM SONGS

"Oh, What a Forward Young Man
You Are," performed with Marion
Marshall, Joyce McKenzie,
Barbara Smith, and Dan Dailey

Top: *Marion Marshall, Joyce McKenzie, and Barbara Smith were MM's fellow showgirls in her second color film.* Bottom: *Here they join Dan Dailey for this unsubtly colorized publicity shot.*

THE FILMS OF MARILYN MONROE

THE FIREBALL

Marilyn, James Brown, and Mickey Rooney light up this colorized lobby card.

Pinning back her long hair, MM seems ever-willing to satisfy the requirements of the studio publicity machine.

STORYLINE

Struggling on his own after running away from Father O'Hara's orphanage, Johnny Casar lands a job in a small restaurant. He attends a roller bowl where he meets roller-skating champion Mary Reeves, who trains him in the art of skating on wheels. After progressing to the point where he is able to outstrip ace skater Mack Miller, Johnny is recruited by the Bears, the Roller Derby champions. Success on the rink and popularity with the crowds soon go to his head. He increasingly spends his work time showing off his individual skills and his leisure hours in the company of groupies such as Polly. Yet, it is Mary who nurses Johnny back to health after he has contracted polio, a tragedy that teaches him a sobering lesson. Regaining his health, Johnny returns to action with the Bears, eventually revealing a more likable side. Rather than stealing the limelight for himself during the International—the biggest match of the season—he helps a colleague win the race for the team.

BEHIND THE SCENES

Originally titled *The Challenge, The Fireball* was a Mickey Rooney vehicle designed to cash in on the Roller Derby craze sweeping America during this time. Rooney, best known for his series of musicals with Judy Garland, had been a top box-office attraction as a teenager. By 1950, he was still a young man, but his career was in sharp decline. He kept afloat by starring in low-budget independent films, among other ventures.

An independent production released through Fox, *The Fireball* was filmed during January and February of 1950, a time when Johnny Hyde was having difficulty persuading producers to audition Marilyn for important roles. The film was not released until later that year. By that time she had appeared on screens in her breakthrough movie, *The Asphalt Jungle,* and been working in another landmark drama, *All About Eve.* From the standpoint of Marilyn's career, the release at this juncture of *The Fireball*—a low-budget vehicle for a star on the decline—seems like poor timing.

CAST

Johnny Casar . . . .Mickey Rooney
Father O'Hara . . . .Pat O'Brien
Mary Reeves . . . .Beverly Tyler
Mack Miller . . .Glenn Corbett
Allen . . . . . . .James Brown
Polly . . . . . .Marilyn Monroe
Bruno Crystal . . .Ralph Dumke
Shilling. . . . . . .Bert Begley
Jeff Davis . . . .Milburn Stone
Dr. Barton . . . . . .Tom Flint
Ullman . . . . . .John Hedloe

CREDITS

A Twentieth Century-Fox release
of a Thor Production

Produced by Bert Friedlob

Directed by Tay Garnett

Screenplay by Tay Garnett and
Horace McCoy

Photographed by Lester White

Art direction by Van Nest Polglase

Music by Victor Young

Released October 1950

*Johnny Hyde's ingenue, happy
with life in Hollywood.*

Top: *By 1950, Mickey Rooney (right, alongside James Brown,) was a 30-year-old veteran of more
than 120 films.* Bottom: *Yet, he was still boyish enough for a juvenile role opposite Pat O'Brien.*

THE FILMS OF MARILYN MONROE

THE ASPHALT JUNGLE

In 1950, Marilyn's face still had more publicity value than her name.

"Some sweet kid!" Alonzo D. Emmerich (Louis Calhern) admires the tender smile of his "niece," Angela Phinlay (MM).

STORYLINE

Doc Riedenschneider emerges from prison with plans to rob a jewelry store. He recruits Dix Handley, Gus Minissi, and Louis Ciavelli as his assistants, while Cobby the bookmaker agrees to provide the finances for the operation. Lawyer Alonzo D. Emmerich is to act as the fence by purchasing the stolen jewels in order to avert police suspicion. The heist is successful, but after the burglar alarm is triggered, a struggle with the night watchman results in Louis being shot. The gang's luck turns increasingly sour when Doc and Dix try to deliver the jewels to Emmerich. They discover that he is broke and has been planning a double cross. One of Emmerich's aides pulls a gun and demands the loot, but he is shot dead by Dix, who is seriously wounded during the exchange. The body of the dead henchman provides a vital clue to the police. After arresting Cobby, they catch up with Emmerich at the home of his naive, young "niece" (i.e. mistress), Angela Phinlay. Her failure to back up his alibi leads to his arrest, followed by those of Gus and Doc, while Louis and Dix die as a result of their wounds.

BEHIND THE SCENES

After months of touting Marilyn's talents, Johnny Hyde, together with MGM casting director Lucille Ryman, finally landed her an audition with noted director John Huston for a small but key role in his crime drama *The Asphalt Jungle*. Marilyn spent three days and nights working studiously with Natasha Lytess to prepare for the reading. For her audition, Marilyn asked Huston if she could recline on the floor as part of her interpretation of the character, and he agreed. Not satisfied with her first reading, she asked to do it again, though Huston had already decided to give her the role.

Marilyn's youthfully seductive performance as Angela provided the first glimpse of her improvement as an actress since *Ladies of the Chorus*. The role was the breakthrough that she had been waiting for. The reviewer for *The People* was moved to comment, "Marilyn Monroe would fetch the wolves out of any jungle, asphalt or otherwise."

Dix Handley. . . .Sterling Hayden
Alonzo D. Emmerich . . . . . .
. . . . .Louis Calhern
Doll Conovan . . . .Jean Hagen
Doc Erwin Riedenschneider . . .
. . . . .Sam Jaffe
Gus Minissi. . .James Whitmore
Police Commissioner Hardy . . .
. . . . .John McIntire
Cobby. . . . . .Marc Lawrence
Lieutenant Dietrich. . . . . .
. . . . Barry Kelley
Louis Ciavelli . .Anthony Caruso
Maria Ciavelli . . . .Teresa Celli
Angela Phinlay . . . .
. . . . . . .Marilyn Monroe
Timmons . . . .William Davis
May Emmerich . . .Dorothy Tree
Bob Brannom. . . .Brad Dexter
Dr. Swanson . . . .John Maxwell
Janocek . . . . . . James Seay
James X. Connery . . . . . .
. . . .Thomas Browne Henry
Andrews . . . . .Don Haggerty
Jeannie . . . . .Helene Stanley
Franz Schurz . . .Henry Rowland
Tallboy . . . . .Raymond Roe

CREDITS

Metro-Goldwyn-Mayer

Produced by Arthur Hornblow, Jr.

Directed by John Huston

Screenplay by Ben Maddow and
John Huston

From a novel by W.R. Burnett

Photographed by Harold Rosson

Art direction by Cedric Gibbons
and Randall Duell

Music by Miklos Rozsa

Released June 1950

Top: *MM once said that* The Asphalt Jungle *contained her finest dramatic performance.* Bottom: *She described director John Huston as "a genius—the first I had ever met."*

THE FILMS OF MARILYN MONROE

CAST

Margo Channing. . .Bette Davis
Eve Harrington . . .Anne Baxter
Addison DeWitt. . . . .
. . . . . . .George Sanders
Karen Richards . .Celeste Holm
Bill Sampson . . . .Gary Merrill
Lloyd Richards . .Hugh Marlowe
Birdie . . . . . .Thelma Ritter
Miss Caswell . .Marilyn Monroe
Max Fabian . . .Gregory Ratoff
Phoebe. . . . . .Barbara Bates
Aged Actor. . .Walter Hampden
Girl . . . . . . .Randy Stuart
Leading Man . . . .Craig Hill
Doorman . . . .Leland Harris
Autograph Seeker . . . . . .
. . . . . . .Barbara White
Stage Manager . . .Eddie Fisher
Clerk . . . . . .William Pullen
Pianist . . . . .Claude Stroud
Frenchman . . . .Eugene Borden
Captain of Waiters. . . . . .
. . . . .Steven Geray

CREDITS

Twentieth Century-Fox

Produced by Darryl F. Zanuck

Directed and written by
Joseph L. Mankiewicz

From the story "The Wisdom of
Eve" by Mary Orr

Photographed by Milton Krasner

Art direction by Lloyd Wheeler
and George W. Davis

Music by Alfred Newman

Released November 1950

For All About Eve, *MM's hair was dyed golden blonde. Her makeup was applied by Allan "Whitey" Snider, who regularly enhanced her appearance on the screen from 1946 to 1962.*

THE FILMS OF MARILYN MONROE

ALL ABOUT EVE

Celebrated stage actress Margo Channing falls for young Eve Harrington's hard-luck story and employs her as a secretary. But Eve is a ruthlessly ambitious actress who is using her employer to further her own career. Margo's suspicions are not aroused until she throws a party for her show-business friends and watches as Eve shamelessly promotes herself. Margo is the only one who sees Eve's true colors. Margo's friends and coworkers are taken in by the aspiring young actress, and they chastise Margo for treating her badly. Using charm, threats, and betrayal, Eve maneuvers her way into the position of understudy for Margo. One night, she goes on for the aging actress when two well-meaning but naive friends conspire to keep Margo away from the theater so that Eve can have her big break. Eventually, Eve lands a role intended for Margo after the older performer retires, and the conniving ingenue becomes Broadway's newest star. Throughout these backstage maneuverings, sharp-tongued critic Addison DeWitt has been keeping an astute eye on Eve and her underhanded tactics. When the right moment comes, she plays straight into his hands. She foolishly informs him of her plan to land great roles by convincing playwright Lloyd Richards to divorce his wife and marry her. DeWitt responds by cooly threatening to reveal Eve's sordid past, thereby claiming her for himself. The irony of Eve's situation is complete after she receives the Sarah Siddons Award for her performance in her latest play. A young fan awaits the star when she returns to her hotel room after the awards ceremony. The girl professes to be a great fan while Eve seems absorbed in her moment of glory. While Eve is out of the room, the young fan poses in front of a mirror with the award. Is history about to repeat itself?

A color-tinted lobby card for a legendary black & white film.

MM sits with a book on heart disease—timely reading matter in light of Johnny Hyde's soon-to-be fatal malady.

BEHIND THE SCENES

As a result of Marilyn's performance in *The Asphalt Jungle*, Johnny Hyde persuaded director Joseph Mankiewicz to cast her in a small but significant role in *All About Eve*, which would eventually win six Academy Awards, including best picture.

Marilyn, an avid reader, took a "Backgrounds in Literature" course at UCLA in 1951.

In this classic drama of backstage machinations, Marilyn portrayed an empty-headed actress named Miss Caswell, who is Addison DeWitt's party companion described by the inimitable DeWitt as "a student of the Copacabana School of Dramatic Art." Though she appeared in only a handful of scenes, Marilyn attracted the attention of her coworkers.

Celeste Holm, who played Margo's friend, Karen, in the film, was initially irritated by Marilyn's habitual lateness in showing up on the set, but this did not cloud the opinion of Russian character actor Gregory Ratoff. Holm recalled, "About the third day, Mr. Ratoff said, 'That girl is going to be beeeg star!' I said, 'Why, because she keeps everyone waiting?' And he said, 'No, she has a quality.' Well, I saw this soft and vulnerable quality, but I didn't know how much will was behind it, I didn't know how much drive."

While watching the daily rushes, Darryl F. Zanuck, who was the studio head at Twentieth Century-Fox, also noticed a special quality about Marilyn. After viewing her in a screen test—her second for Fox—he re-signed the struggling actress for another six-month term. An underling reminded Zanuck that Marilyn Monroe had been under contract with Fox once before and dropped. The powerful studio executive roared, "I don't care. Bring her back."

As negotiated by Johnny Hyde, the new contract was implemented on December 10, 1950. Hyde died eight days later.

Above and right: *Agent Johnny Hyde successfully shaped Marilyn for stardom.*

GEORGE SANDERS

Born to British parents on July 3, 1906, in St. Petersburg, Russia, Sanders most often played the cultivated yet cynical scoundrel. He and Marilyn reportedly had an affair during the making of the picture, though he was married to Zsa Zsa Gabor, the second of his four wives. His 1960 autobiography, Memoirs of a Professional Cad, *seemed appropriately titled. On April 25, 1972, he returned to his hotel room after an interview on Spanish TV and wrote a farewell note explaining he was bored with life "in this sweet cesspool." He then took his own life by overdosing on sleeping pills.*

Top left: *MM with Bette Davis and George Sanders, who won an Oscar for his role.* Bottom left: *(From left) Gregory Ratoff, Anne Baxter, Gary Merrill, Sanders, Celeste Holm (top), and MM (bottom).*

RIGHT CROSS

In 1950, Marilyn had two tiny blemishes on her chin surgically removed.

Right Cross *was the second of Marilyn's three films for MGM.*

STORYLINE

Champion prizefighter Johnny Monterez is tied to fading promoter Sean O'Malley because he is in love with the old man's daughter, Pat. When he realizes that a weak right hand threatens his career, Johnny decides to sign up with top promoter Allan Goff. He hopes to quickly net enough money to support both Pat and her father. After learning that his only client is going to leave him, O'Malley dies of heart failure. Pat blames Johnny for her father's death, unaware of her boyfriend's honorable intentions. Johnny, in turn, stakes his title on one last fight for the O'Malley organization, a bout that is expected to attract a large crowd. Johnny's luck goes from bad to worse when he loses the fight and breaks his hand in a dressing room brawl with his friend, reporter Rick Gavery. When Pat uncovers the real reason Johnny switched promoters, she and Rick follow him to his training camp to patch up their differences. Johnny's career in the ring has come to an end, but his life with Pat is just beginning.

BEHIND THE SCENES

Marilyn's role in *Right Cross*, as Rick's girlfriend in a nightclub scene, was so small that she remained unbilled on most cast lists circulated in reviews. Her character, Dusky Ledoux, *was* referred to by name in the film, though Marilyn speaks only a few insignificant lines in her single scene.

During this erratic period, Marilyn gained additional public exposure by way of her one and only television commercial in which she promoted Union Oil's Royal Triton gasoline in the suggestive manner that was fast becoming her forte. "This is the first car I ever owned," she tells the men who have just pushed her vehicle into the gas station. "I call it Cynthia. She's going to have the best care a car ever had."

Turning to the pump attendant, Marilyn orders him to "Put Royal Triton in Cynthia's little tummy." She then looks straight into the camera, and, with her characteristic wide eyes and lowered upper lip, she breathily informs California viewers, "Cynthia will just love that Royal Triton!"

Marilyn excelled at publicity.

Top: *One of the two male stars was Dick Powell, who had turned from musical comedy crooner to dramatic actor.* Bottom: *The other was Mexican-born actor Ricardo Montalban (with raised fists).*

HOMETOWN STORY

Miss Iris Martin (MM)... no ordinary, run-of-the-mill office secretary!

Hometown Story—a flat, unexceptional movie except for the presence of Marilyn.

STORYLINE

After Blake Washburn is defeated by John MacFarland, the son of a wealthy manufacturer, in a state legislature election, he becomes obsessed with the idea that big business is not only responsible for a lot of society's problems but also his own unemployment. He returns to his hometown to take over as editor of the local newspaper, called the *Herald*. As the editor, he begins campaigning against high finance in general and MacFarland in particular. When Blake's kid sister, Katie, is badly injured in a mine-shaft accident during a school trip, MacFarland commissions a plane to rush her to a hospital after she has been examined by his company doctor. When brain surgery and a respirator running on a MacFarland company motor save Katie's life, Blake changes his views on big business.

BEHIND THE SCENES

An industrial film that was not intended for general release, *Hometown Story* is simplistic propaganda. Sponsored and supervised by John K. Ford, head of General Motors' film division, this superficial melodrama was designed to promote American industry and criticize liberal views of big business.

Hometown Story was Marilyn's third and final project for MGM, and it was produced, directed, and written by Arthur Pierson, who had directed Marilyn in *Dangerous Years*. Production was completed just prior to her new contract with Fox, making it the last movie she acted in before the death of her mentor, Johnny Hyde, on December 18, 1950.

As a bit player, Marilyn was often expected to provide her own wardrobe. The sweater with the gray body and black sleeves that she wore in her role as Miss Martin, the secretary in *Hometown Story*, had been worn earlier in the year for her role as Polly in *The Fireball* and in her final scene in *All About Eve*. She also wore this same sweater-skirt ensemble in the screen test she was required to take before being offered her contract at Fox. Though some have suggested that Marilyn did this for good luck, it could also have been a matter of low funds.

CAST

Blake Washburn . . .Jeffrey Lynn
John MacFarland . .Donald Crisp
Janice Hunt . .Marjorie Reynolds
Slim Haskins . . .Alan Hale, Jr.
Iris Martin . . .Marilyn Monroe
Mrs. Washburn . .Barbara Brown
Katie Washburn . . . .
. . . . . . .Melinda Plowman
Uncle Cliff. . . . .Griff Barnett
Taxi Driver. . . .Kenny McEvoy
Kenlock . . . . . .Glenn Tryon
Berny Miles . . . .Byron Foulger
Phoebe Hartman. . . . .
. . . . .Virginia Campbell
Andy Butterworth . . . .
. . . . .Harry Harvey
Dr. Johnson . . . .Nelson Leigh
Motorcycle Officer . . . .
. . . . .Speck Noblitt

CREDITS

Metro-Goldwyn-Mayer

Produced, directed, and written
by Arthur Pierson

Photographed by Lucien Andriot

Art direction by Hilyard Brown

Music by Louis Forbes

Released May 1951

Top: *In her third and final film for MGM, Marilyn appeared opposite Alan Hale, Jr.* Bottom and right: *Prior to beginning her second Fox contract, MM still modeled on a regular basis.*

AS YOUNG AS YOU FEEL

Marilyn's first film under her new Fox contract: MM is prominently featured in image if not by name.

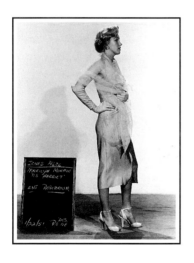

A wardrobe test showing a profile of a slightly "bulbous" nose. Though unsubstantiated, many believe she had this surgically corrected about 1950.

STORYLINE

Company policy forces John Hodges to retire at the age of 65 from his job at Acme Printing Services, a subsidiary of Consolidated Motors, but he is determined not to take it lying down. When Hodges discovers no one seems to know what the president of Consolidated—whose name is Cleveland—looks like, the crafty senior dyes his hair and beard black to look younger, and then poses as the top man. His disguise is good enough to fool Louis McKinley, the puffed-up president of Acme, into arranging an inspection tour and dinner for him. During dinner, "Mr. Cleveland" announces a new policy granting all employees who are retired the opportunity to return to their jobs. This kind-hearted gesture impresses many people, including the company stockholders, McKinley's love-starved wife, Lucille, and the real Cleveland, who immediately pays Hodges a visit. Having left her fatheaded husband, Lucille McKinley also arrives on the doorstep of the phony Mr. Cleveland. When McKinley shows up to retrieve her, he unwittingly fires the real company president. McKinley then faints on learning what he has done, while Hodges is reinstated to his former position.

BEHIND THE SCENES

Though Marilyn's amusing role was essentially decorative, Fox's publicity material for *As Young As You Feel* indicated that the studio knew it had a hot property because it was MM who was featured most prominently on the film's posters. Promotional handouts informed moviegoers that "the azure-eyed, honey-tressed actress with the most provocative chassis to reach the screen since Jean Harlow, has five wardrobe changes—each a sweater of a different type . . . described by the costuming department as: 1. Loose fitting 2. Draping 3. Clinging 4. Tight 5. Gee whizz!!!"

At the very bottom of the cast list was 22-year-old Roger Moore—the future James Bond—who was popping up in only his second film after graduating from London's Royal Academy of Dramatic Art.

CAST

John Hodges . . . .Monty Woolley
Della Hodges . . .Thelma Ritter
Joe Elliott . . . . .David Wayne
Alice Hodges. . . . .Jean Peters
Lucille McKinley . . . .
. . . . . .Constance Bennett
Harriet . . . . .Marilyn Monroe
George Hodges . . .Allyn Joslyn
Louis McKinley . .Albert Dekker
Frank Erickson . . . .
. . . . . . .Clinton Sundberg
Cleveland. . . . .Minor Watson
Conductor . . . .Ludwig Stossel
Harpist . . . . . .Renie Riano
Gallagher . . . . .Wally Brown
Willie . . . . . .Rusty Tamblyn
Saltonstall . . . . .Roger Moore

CREDITS

Twentieth Century-Fox

Produced and written by
Lamar Trotti

Directed by Harmon Jones

Based on a story by
Paddy Chayefsky

Photographed by
Joseph MacDonald

Art direction by Lyle Wheeler and
Maurice Ransford

Music by Cyril Mockridge

Released June 1951

Top: *Marilyn's increased stature meant more lines to exchange with stars such as Albert Dekker.*
Bottom: *She could also count on extra scenes such as this one with Jean Peters and David Wayne.*

THE FILMS OF MARILYN MONROE

CAST

Connie Scott. . . . .June Haver
Jim Scott . . .William Lundigan
Charley Patterson . . .Frank Fay
Roberta Stevens . . . .
. . . . . . .Marilyn Monroe
Ed Forbes. . . . . .Jack Paar
Eadie Gaynor . . . .Leatrice Joy
George Thompson. .Henry Kulky
Mrs. Quigg. . . . .Marie Blake
Florence . . . . .Patricia Miller
Mrs. Arnold . . .Maude Wallace
Mr. Hansen. . . . .Joe Ploski
Mrs. Thompson . . . .
. . . . . . .Martha Wentworth
Mrs. Frazier . . . .Faire Binney
Mrs. McNab. . . .Caryl Lincoln
Mr. McNab . . . .Michael Ross
Mr. Fain . . . . .Bob Jellison
Postman. . . . .John Costello
Mr. Knowland . .Charles Calvert
Detective Donovan . .Leo Clary
Mr. Clark. . . . . .Jack Daly
Mr. Gray. . . .Ray Montgomery
Mrs. Braddock. . .Florence Auer
Mrs. Engstrand . .Edna Holland
Mrs. Healy . . . . .Liz Slifer
Glazier . . . .Alvin Hammer

CREDITS

Twentieth Century-Fox
Produced by Jules Buck
Directed by Joseph Newman
Screenplay by I.A.L. Diamond
Based on a novel by Scott Corbett
Photographed by Lloyd Ahern
Art direction by Lyle Wheeler and
George L. Patrick
Music by Cyril Mockridge
Released October 1951

Nuzzling up to costar and future TV personality Jack Paar, who would later opine, "Beneath the facade of Marilyn there was only a frightened waitress in a diner."

LOVE NEST

After completing his military service overseas, Jim Scott wants only to settle down in New York City with his wife, Connie, and write a novel. However, problems with the rundown apartment building that Connie purchased just before his discharge thwart his plans, as does the arrival of Jim's glamorous army pal, ex-WAC Roberta "Bobbie" Stevens. Both place undue strain on the budding novelist's career and the Scotts' marriage. Matters are further complicated when Jim accepts money for refurbishments from one of his tenants, Charley Patterson. Charley is actually a likable but larcenous con man who earns a living by securing money from rich widows on the promise of investing it for them. Subsequently arrested and jailed, Charley tells the police that his landlord is in possession of hush money, prompting Jim's own arrest and providing Charley with the opportunity to put together another get-rich-quick scheme. With the two of them stuck behind bars in the city jail, Charley relates his memoirs to Jim, which are to be serialized in a popular magazine. The writer's fee will be equally divided between the Scotts and Charley's recent bride, Eadie. Released as soon as Charley tells the police that the young landlord is innocent, Jim turns the old con man's story into a biography. Profits from the best-seller provide enough money for the Scotts to renovate their apartment building and Eadie to subsist until she is reunited with her husband. Released 14 months later, Charley and Eadie surprise everyone by having twins.

B E H I N D   T H E   S C E N E S

While *Love Nest* provided Marilyn with a meatier role—that of a potential home-wrecker—it was an offscreen incident that gave the struggling actress the professional stability and financial security she had worked so long and hard for.

The comedy began shooting under the working title *A WAC in His Life* in April of 1951. During production, the studio threw an exhibitors' party

This domestic farce was one of the many Fox comedies that required the services of a buxom blonde.

Shapely Bobbie Stevens (MM) transforms the Scotts' marital bliss into marital blitz.

at the Cafe de Paris, commonly known as the Twentieth Century-Fox commissary. Many studio executives and big-name stars were in attendance, including Susan Hayward, Gregory Peck, Anne Baxter, June Haver (the female lead in *Love Nest*), and Tyrone Power. Yet, when Marilyn—a mere starlet—arrived one-and-a-half hours late, all eyes were immediately drawn towards the breathless blonde in a black, strapless cocktail gown. Aware of the impact, Fox president Spyros Skouras (once described by director Billy Wilder as "the only Greek tragedy I know") took her by the arm and sat her down by his side at the head table.

The next morning, following Skouras's reasoning that, "If the exhibitors like her, the public likes her," production chief Darryl F. Zanuck arranged a new seven-year contract for "the most exciting new personality in Hollywood in a long time." Commencing on May 11, 1951, this latest contract raised Marilyn's salary to $500 a week. It also meant that by the time *Love Nest* was released in October, she was billed fourth. She was the subject of a massive publicity build-up that included a cover shot on *Look* magazine, an appearance in *Life* magazine, and an interview in *Collier's*, in which she mused, "Someday I want to have a house of my own with trees and grass and hedges all around, but never trim them at all—just let them grow any old way they want."

During the next few months the studio cast her in any Fox film that required a sexy blonde. Hollywood was far more interested in Marilyn's value in terms of her looks than in her talent as an actress. As her *Love Nest* costar (and future television personality) Jack Paar later observed, "Looking back, I guess I should have been excited, but I found her pretty tiresome. She used to carry around books by Marcel Proust with their titles facing out; but I never saw her read one. She was always holding up shooting by talking on the phone. Judging from what's happened, though, I guess she had the right number."

Top: *Renie's costume designs for the film were sober but sophisticated.* Bottom: *But, Marilyn could lend sexiness and class to whatever she wore.*

Wardrobe test for the kind of nightwear that MM would never have worn in real life.

Top left: *Former silent star Leatrice Joy (above Marilyn) in her last film.* Bottom left: *June Haver in her penultimate appearance before serving briefly as a nun, then marrying Fred MacMurray.*

LET'S MAKE IT LEGAL

Macdonald Carey starred as habitual gambler Hugh Halsworth.

A color-tinted Marilyn posing in the gold bathing suit that she wore in the movie.

STORYLINE

Hugh and Miriam Halsworth's decision to separate after 20 years of marriage had more to do with their bickering than with any loss of affection. Consequently, each tries to make the other one jealous. Hugh dates a sensual blonde named Joyce, while Miriam rekindles her relationship with her first love, Victor Macfarland. Miriam had only married Hugh after she had been inexplicably deserted by Victor. After all of these years, she discovers why Victor had left her. It seems that Hugh, an inveterate gambler, had won her hand on a roll of the dice. Miriam is so hurt by this discovery that she agrees to marry Victor. She irritates Hugh even further by threatening to destroy his beloved rose bushes. His attempt to rescue the flowers leads to his arrest. When a newspaper story details the unfortunate incident, Victor complains bitterly about seeing his good name smeared just because he happens to be Miriam's fiancé. His selfishness makes her realize that she is far happier in the arms of her husband.

BEHIND THE SCENES

Though she had just 14 lines in a 113-page script, MM nevertheless attracted the attention of her costars with a burgeoning reputation for arriving late on the set. Matters came to a head when director Richard Sale lambasted Marilyn in front of cast and crew for keeping everyone waiting. Sale demanded an apology from her. She refused and stormed off the set, threatening to involve her close friend Joseph Schenck, Fox's president, in the dispute. After a few minutes, cooler heads prevailed, and Marilyn returned to apologize, thanking Sale in the process for "straightening" her out.

Originally titled *Don't Call Me Mother*, the comedy also featured Robert Wagner. On June 14, 1951, he had appeared opposite Marilyn in his screen test for Fox. Later he recalled that for Marilyn, "It just didn't all happen real easy . . . It took a lot of time, a lot of rehearsing to create that whole image and to create that wonderful sort of thing that she did . . . She was a very lonely person, and one sensed that."

CAST

Miriam Halsworth . . . .
. . . . . . .Claudette Colbert
Hugh Halsworth . . . .
. . . . . . .Macdonald Carey
Victor Macfarland . . . .
. . . . .Zachary Scott
Barbara Denham. .Barbara Bates
Jerry Denham . .Robert Wagner
Joyce . . . . . .Marilyn Monroe
Ferguson . . . . . .Frank Cady
Gardener . . . . .Jim Hayward
Miss Jessup. . . . .Carol Savage
Milkman . . . . . .Paul Gerrits
Secretary . . .Betty Jane Bowen
Hugh's Secretary. . . .Vici Raaf
Police Lieutenant. . . . . . .
. . . . .Ralph Sanford
Hotel Manager . . .Harry Denny
Postman . . . .Harry Harvey, Sr.

CREDITS

Twentieth Century-Fox

Produced by Robert Bassler

Directed by Richard Sale

Screenplay by F. Hugh Herbert
and I.A.L. Diamond

Story by Mortimer Braus

Photographed by Lucien Ballard

Art Direction by Lyle Wheeler
and Albert Hogsett

Music by Cyril Mockridge

Released November 1951

Top: *MM plays cards on the set with some supporting players in between scenes.* Bottom: *Hamming it up in front of the cameras with Macdonald Carey, Zachary Scott, and Claudette Colbert.*

CLASH BY NIGHT

A melodramatic insert promoting the movie, which was produced by Harriet Parsons, daughter of powerful Hollywood columnist Louella Parsons.

STORYLINE

After ten wasted years of searching for happiness in the big city, Mae Doyle grudgingly resigns herself to a more sedate life in her small home town, where she settles down with Jerry D'Amato, a kindly but plain fishing boat skipper, and their newborn baby. Mae soon grows bored, however, particularly after the arrival of Jerry's handsome friend, Earl, who reminds her of the passion and excitement she once wanted. Mae and Earl, a self-pitying soul who works as a film projectionist, embark on an affair. When Jerry learns of their relationship, he explodes, almost killing Earl before boarding his boat with the baby. Mae realizes the mistake she has made when Earl tries to persuade her to leave the child behind and run away with him. Instead, she runs after Jerry and begs his forgiveness. The couple realize they still love one another, and Jerry agrees to give her another chance.

BEHIND THE SCENES

When RKO borrowed Marilyn from Fox for *Clash by Night*, little did they realize the value behind the deal they were making. Before the film's release, newspapers revealed that Marilyn was the nude girl on the well-known "Golden Dreams" calendar. Wire service reporter Aline Mosby broke the story, informing excited readers that MM had posed nude for photographer Tom Kelley back in 1949. Opinions vary as to who actually tipped Mosby off. Some have suggested that it was the film's producers, Jerry Wald and Norman Krasna, looking for free publicity. Others speculate that Marilyn herself revealed the information. Either way, when the Fox executives were faced with press inquiries, they instructed their rising starlet to deny everything. But Marilyn chose her own path. With the support of Fox publicity director, Harry Brand, Marilyn admitted her indiscretion but felt no need to apologize for it. The result was that a potent combination of public sympathy and titillation led to a massive increase in MM's fan mail—and tremendous box-office receipts for *Clash by Night*.

CAST

Mae Doyle. . . .Barbara Stanwyck
Jerry D'Amato . . . .Paul Douglas
Earl Pfeiffer . . . . .Robert Ryan
Peggy . . . . .Marilyn Monroe
Uncle Vince. . . .J. Carrol Naish
Joe Doyle . . . . .Keith Andes
Papa . . . . . .Silvio Minciotti

CREDITS

An RKO release of a
Jerry Wald–Norman Krasna
Production

Produced by Harriet Parsons

Directed by Fritz Lang

Screenplay by Alfred Hayes

Based on the play by
Clifford Odets

Photographed by
Nicholas Musuraca

Art Direction by Albert
D'Agostino and Carroll Clark

Music by Roy Webb

Released June 1952

Top: *MM's calendar-related popularity with the press exploded during the shooting of* Clash. *Bottom: This led to the resentment of coworkers including Paul Douglas (center, between MM and Keith Andes).*

Marilyn in a clinch with her love interest in the film, Keith Andes.

WE'RE NOT MARRIED

Colorized lobby card for the only completed movie featuring Marilyn as a mother.

Wardrobe test for yet another role requiring very little in the way of costume material.

S T O R Y L I N E

Justice of the Peace Melvin Bush performs a series of weddings without realizing that his new license has not yet become valid. When the error is discovered, five couples receive letters informing them that they are not legally married. Among them are Jeff Norris and his "wife," Annabel, who is the reigning Mrs. Mississippi. Annabel has been spending more time parading her charms in a swimsuit than taking care of her husband and baby. Jeff is delighted by the letter because this means she is no longer eligible for the Mrs. America contest, but his celebration is cut short when Annabel happily announces that she is now in the running for the title of Miss Mississippi! Annable wins, and afterwards all three members of the Norris family participate in a second marriage ceremony.

B E H I N D   t h e   S C E N E S

While Otis L. Guernsey, Jr., of the *New York Herald Tribune* maintained that Marilyn "looks as though she had been carved out of cake by Michelangelo," the publicity for *We're Not Married* emphasized both MM and Zsa Zsa Gabor, calling them America's "dreamgirls." The movie consisted of five separate episodes, each focusing on one of the hapless couples who discover they are not really wed. Interestingly, Marilyn and Zsa Zsa never actually appear on-screen together. That was just as well, because there was little love lost between them—a situation stemming primarily from Zsa Zsa's resentment over the attention husband George Sanders paid to Marilyn during the shooting of *All About Eve*.

What did cause friction during production was a new habit Marilyn had begun during the shooting of *Clash by Night*. Insecure Marilyn refused to shoot a scene unless Natasha Lytess was allowed on the set to assist her. "Her habit of looking at me the second she finished a scene was to become a joke in projection rooms," Lytess later revealed. "The film of the daily rushes was filled with scenes of Marilyn, finishing her dialogue and immediately shading her eyes to find me, to see if she had done well."

CAST

Ramona . . . . . .Ginger Rogers
Steve Gladwyn . . . .Fred Allen
Melvin Bush . . . .Victor Moore
Annabel Norris . . . .
. . . . . . .Marilyn Monroe
Jeff Norris . . . . .David Wayne
Katie Woodruff. . . .Eve Arden
Hector Woodruff . .Paul Douglas
Willie Fisher . . .Eddie Bracken
Patsy Fisher . . . .Mitzi Gaynor
Freddie Melrose . .Louis Calhern
Eve Melrose . . .Zsa Zsa Gabor
Duffy . . . . .James Gleason
Attorney Stone . . .Paul Stewart
Mrs. Bush . . . . .Jane Darwell
Detective Magnus . .Alan Bridge
Radio Announcer . .Harry Golder
Governor Bush . . . .
. . . . . .Victor Sutherland
Attorney General. . .Tom Powers
Organist . . . . .Maurice Cass
Autograph Hound . . . . . .
. . . . . . .Maude Wallace
Irene . . . . . .Margie Liszt
Mr. Graves . . .Richard Buckley
Pinky . . . . . .Lee Marvin

CREDITS

Twentieth Century-Fox

Produced and written by
Nunnally Johnson

Directed by Edmund Goulding

Screenplay adapted by
Dwight Taylor

From a story by Gina Kaus and
Jay Dratler

Photographed by Leo Tover

Art Direction by Lyle Wheeler
and Leland Fuller

Music by Cyril Mockridge

Released July 1952

Top: *Annabel (MM), Jeff (David Wayne), and Duffy (James Gleason) learn that Jeff and Annabel's marriage is invalid.* Bottom: *But all ends well, as illustrated in this colorized lobby-card photo.*

THE FILMS OF MARILYN MONROE

CAST

Jed Towers . . .	.Richard Widmark
Nell	.Marilyn Monroe
Lyn Leslie . . .	.Anne Bancroft
Bunny Jones. .	.Donna Corcoran
Rochelle	.Jeanne Cagney
Mrs. Ruth Jones .	.Lurene Tuttle
Eddie	.Elisha Cook, Jr.
Peter Jones	.Jim Backus
Mrs. Ballew . . .	.Verna Felton
Bartender . .	.Willis B. Bouchey
Girl Photographer	
. . . . . .	.Gloria Blondell
Mr. Ballew	.Don Beddoe
Mrs. McMurdock .	.Grace Hayle
Pat the House Detective	
. . . .	.Michael Ross
Maid	.Eda Reis Merin
Elevator Operator .	.Victor Perrin
Bell Captain . . .	.Dick Cogan
Doorman	.Robert Foulk
Desk Clerk	.Olan Soule
Toastmaster . . .	.Emmett Vogan

CREDITS

Twentieth Century-Fox

Produced by Julian Blaustein

Directed by Roy Baker

Screenplay by Daniel Taradash

Based on a novel by
Charlotte Armstrong

Photographed by Lucien Ballard

Art Direction by Lyle Wheeler
and Richard Irvine

Music directed by Lionel Newman

Released August 1952

*Marilyn reverted to unbleached, dark blonde hair for this dramatic portrayal, which, according to
critic Bosley Crowther, utilized "a childishly blank expression and a provokingly feeble, hollow voice."*

DON'T BOTHER
TO KNOCK

STORYLINE

Hired by Mr. and Mrs. Peter Jones to baby-sit for their daughter, Bunny, the attractive but lonely Nell arrives at their hotel suite with the help of her uncle, Eddie the elevator operator. After the Joneses have departed, Nell's potentially boring evening is brightened by Jed Towers, a hard-boiled airline pilot who has seen Nell from his bedroom window. Jed has just broken up with his girlfriend, Lyn Leslie, a singer at the same hotel, but little time elapses before he arranges to meet Nell. Even less time is necessary for him to realize that Nell has severe psychological problems. Believing that Jed is her long-lost fiancé who was listed as missing in action during World War II, Nell lashes out hysterically at anyone who interrupts her time with him, including Eddie and little Bunny. Jed decides that it is best for him to leave, and Nell blames the child for his hasty exit. After the pilot confides in Lyn about the strange events in Suite 809, he returns to find Bunny tied up and Mrs. Jones grappling with Nell. Jed separates them, but Nell gets away. He finds her in the hotel lobby, threatening to kill herself with a razor. Jed convinces her to hand over the razor and give herself up to the police. The poor, deluded girl realizes her fiancé is dead and agrees to undergo hospital treatment. Lyn, impressed by Jed's compassion for Nell, falls in love with him all over again.

BEHIND THE SCENES

Marilyn moved into the West Hollywood home of her acting coach, Natasha Lytess, in preparation for her role as the emotionally disturbed Nell, which was her first heavily dramatic part. Lytess, whose relationship with Marilyn ended badly, later quipped about her time as MM's roommate, "Marilyn is a moonwalker. When she used to live in my house, I often felt like she was a somnambulist walking around."

Directors were usually none too happy about Lytess walking around their movie sets, and actors were often perturbed about having to reshoot a scene if Marilyn did not receive a nod of approval from her mentor. *Don't*

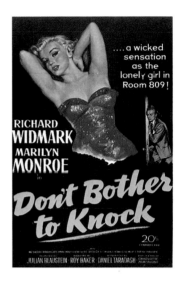

This poster disregards MM's on-screen appearance in the film.

Bunny (Donna Corcoran) looks slightly unsure about the mad glint in the eyes of her babysitter (MM).

Top and bottom: *This was the first of eight movies for which William Travilla designed Marilyn's costumes. He proclaimed her "the easiest person I ever worked with."*

Bother to Knock, however, proved to be the exception to the rule. Reportedly, Marilyn did not require a single retake during production. While she was proud of her performance, this psychological thriller—originally titled *Night Without Sleep* until Fox realized that it had scheduled another movie with the same name—did little to further her career.

Poor, almost laughable dialogue and a heavy-handed approach to the material garnered mixed reviews for the film. Some critics, unable to discern the problems beneath the surface of the film, blamed Marilyn for its weaknesses. Bosley Crowther of *The New York Times* complained, ". . . unfortunately, all the equipment that Miss Monroe has to handle the job are a childishly blank expression and a provokingly feeble, hollow voice." Other critics did their best to sound positive about the performance of the actress whose photo on a nude calendar was still causing a nationwide stir. Archer Winsten of the *New York Post* summed up the situation, "They've thrown Marilyn Monroe into the deep dramatic waters, sink or swim, and while she doesn't really do either, you might say that she floats."

Marilyn's performance as the unstable Nell was effective at times, though the film was poorly handled overall.

ANNE BANCROFT
Making her film debut in Don't Bother to Knock, *Bancroft was profoundly affected by Marilyn's performance in the climactic scene. Bancroft recalled that it was "a remarkable experience. Because it was one of those very few times in all my experiences in Hollywood, when I felt that give and take—that can only happen when you are working with good actors. There was just this one scene of one woman seeing another woman who was helpless and in pain, and she was helpless and in pain. It was so real. . . . She moved me so that tears came into my eyes."*

Top: *Manfully supported by Richard Widmark, MM tried hard to portray a "sick girl."* Bottom: *". . . and she plays the part like a sick girl," asserted critic Philip K. Scheur.*

MONKEY BUSINESS

A poster for the film boasting a stellar collection of talent on both sides of the camera.

While Dr. Barnaby Fulton is experimenting to find a rejuvenation tonic for a drug company, one of his laboratory chimpanzees secretly leaves its cage and mixes a far more effective serum. The chimp's concoction finds its way into a bottle of drinking water, with chaotic results. Both Barnaby and his wife, Edwina, wash down Barnaby's tonic with some of the tainted drinking water, without realizing that it is the latter that is causing their subsequent juvenile behavior. Barnaby, for example, takes off for a swim and some roller skating with his boss's secretary, Lois Laurel. Edwina, thinking she's a young bride, lures her husband to a hotel for a "second honeymoon." Under the influence of the formula, both cause an uproar at an important meeting of the board of directors. After discovering that it is the chimp's mixture that has caused all the mayhem, Barnaby decides to abandon his search for a youth restorative.

BEHIND THE SCENES

Monkey Business originally titled *Darling, I Am Growing Younger*, made up for the temporary career setback of *Don't Bother to Knock* by showcasing Marilyn in a comic role, which was better suited to her talents. Unfortunately, the role was all too familiar to MM. As Kate Cameron of the *New York Daily News* duly noted that "Marilyn Monroe . . . can look and act dumber than any of the screen's current blondes."

By the time *Monkey Business* was released in 1952, Marilyn was rapidly becoming a nationally famous celebrity, and the press began to follow her every move. When she posed with Cary Grant and baseball legend Joe DiMaggio on the set of *Monkey Business*, the photo was reproduced in papers around the country with Grant carefully cropped out, prompting the first rumors of the fairy-tale romance between the beauty and the baseball hero. With this type of media attention, the big time was just around the corner.

Cary Grant admires Marilyn in a costume that, according to Travilla, was one design of his she really detested.

Top and bottom: *In the film, Dr. Barnaby Fulton (Cary Grant) describes Lois Laurel (MM) as being "half child." To which his wife Edwina (Ginger Rogers) counters, "Not the visible half!"*

The film was originally titled Darling, I Am Growing Younger.

THE FILMS OF MARILYN MONROE

O. HENRY'S
FULL HOUSE

A poster for the last movie featuring Marilyn in a non-starring role.

Charles Laughton tries to get on the right side of Marilyn during their brief scene together.

STORYLINE

An anthology consisting of adaptations of five stories by one of America's premier writers, *O. Henry's Full House* utilized the talents of many of Fox's best actors and craftsmen. Each story featured a different cast and was written, directed, and photographed by a different crew. Marilyn starred in the first segment, entitled "The Cop and the Anthem." The story follows the antics of an aristocratic bum named Soapy. With winter about to set in, Soapy settles into his seasonal routine of trying to get arrested so that he can trade the cold outdoors for a cozy home behind bars. This year, however, no matter how hard he tries, his petty crimes do not interest the police. One of his ploys involves accosting a young woman in the hopes that she will scream for help. But, the woman turns out to be a street-walker. Soapy runs away, and the streetwalker is arrested for soliciting. Seeking refuge inside a church, the old bum gets religion and resolves to find decent employment for the first time in his life. But Soapy just cannot win. His good intentions are thwarted when he is arrested for loitering and sentenced to 90 days in jail.

BEHIND THE SCENES

O. Henry's Full House was the last Fox project to feature Marilyn in a second-ary role. It was also the last time that the studio could get away with cast-ing her in such a part—a meaningless walk-on as a prostitute. The part was neither colorful nor comic; nor was it featured in a high-profile film. Clearly the executives at Fox were determined to cash in on her name as much as they could. To this end, publicity material for the film supplied to exhibitors attempted to reassure them that, even though "naturally, Miss Monroe is more at home in a bathing suit," she nevertheless "shows her shape in *O. Henry's Full House* . . . only through two bustles. This is Miss Monroe's first involvement with period costume, and those who have seen the picture report she meets the challenge nobly." And who might this be referring to? The Twentieth Century-Fox accountants?

CREDITS
Twentieth Century-Fox
Produced by Andre Hakim
Music by Lionel Newman
Narrated by John Steinbeck
Released September 1952

MARILYN'S EPISODE

"The Cop and the Anthem"
Directed by Henry Koster
Screenplay by Lamar Trotti
Photographed by Lloyd Ahern

CAST

Soapy . . . . .Charles Laughton
Streetwalker. . .Marilyn Monroe
Horace . . . . . .David Wayne
Man with Umbrella . . . . . .
. . . . .Philip Tonge
Manager .Thomas Browne Henry
Headwaiter . . .Richard Karlan
Waiter . . . . . .Erno Verebes
Judge . . . . . .William Vedder
Bystander. . . . .Billy Wayne
Owner . . . . . . .Nico Lek
Cashier . . . .Marjorie Holliday
Cop . . . . . . .James Flavin

REMAINING
EPISODES

"The Clarion Call,"
starring Richard Widmark
and directed by Henry Hathaway.

"The Last Leaf,"
starring Anne Baxter and
Jean Peters and directed
by Jean Negulesco.

"The Ransom of Red Chief,"
starring Fred Allan and directed
by Howard Hawks.

"The Gift of the Magi,"
starring Jeanne Crain and directed
by Henry King.

Top: *Desperate to get arrested, Soapy (Laughton) goads a young woman (MM) into screaming for help.*
Bottom: *But, on discovering that she is a streetwalker, it is he who panics and flees.*

THE FILMS OF MARILYN MONROE

An advertisement promised: "For sheer power . . . for sheer magnetism . . . the show MARILYN MONROE puts on is as electric and spectacular as Niagara itself!" Clearly, the public agreed.

NIAGARA

Ray and Polly Cutler arrive at Niagara Falls on a belated honeymoon to find that their reserved Rainbow Cabin is already occupied by George and Rose Loomis. The Cutlers take another cabin to avoid trouble, but it soon becomes apparent that relations are strained between the Loomises and trouble is imminent. While visiting the Falls, Polly stumbles across Rose kissing a handsome young man named Ted Patrick, though she says nothing to the suspicious, neurotic George. What Polly does not know is that Rose and Ted are planning to kill George. After George turns up missing, his unfaithful wife notifies the police. Later, Rose is called to the mortuary to identify a dead body, which she fully expects to be her husband. When the sheet is pulled down, she passes out. The real reason for Rose's fainting spell becomes clear when Polly spots George Loomis at the motel and by the Falls. He confides to her that he killed Ted in self-defense—it was his wife's lover under that sheet in the morgue. George tells Polly that he intends to run away. Instead of leaving town, George begins to shadow Rose. She attempts to buy a bus ticket to leave Niagara Falls, but the border between Canada and the States is blocked, and Rose is trapped. George follows the scheming adulteress to the top of the Carillon Tower, where he strangles her. Hijacking the boat that the Cutlers have hired, George makes his escape with Polly trapped on board. Yet, when the vessel is swept into the current of the Falls, George helps Polly climb safely onto a rocky ledge, before he and the boat take a fatal dive over the edge.

BEHIND THE SCENES

"Marilyn Monroe and 'Niagara'—a raging torrent of emotion that even nature can't control!" trumpeted the headline on a poster advertising the movie, and certainly the combined attractions of Marilyn Monroe and the Falls worked their magic at the box office.

Niagara became the film that finally launched Marilyn as a star: the quintessential 1950s seductress, with—from top to bottom—platinum

"Would you mind playing this?" . . . A lobby card illustrates MM selecting "Kiss" to sing along to.

Marilyn, shown murdered for the publicity camera, helps confirm Joseph Cotten's assertion that, "Everything that girl does is sexy."

blonde hair, bedroom eyes, pouting cherry-red lips, a voluptuous chest, and a curvy derriere. Indeed, the latter was featured in its own starring moment in the film. Dressed in a clinging black skirt and bright red sweater, Marilyn walked away from the camera and toward the Falls, rhythmically undulating her hips from side to side. Years of practicing her movie-star walk had paid off for MM, though at the time, the famous 116-foot stroll not only attracted the admiration of many who thought it irresistibly daring but the scorn of others who, in the words of the reviewer for the *Monthly Film Bulletin*, considered Marilyn "vulgar and faintly repulsive."

Marilyn also gained a reputation on the set for being earthy and unconventional, wearing no undergarments, striking provocative poses for the press photographers, and informing journalist Sidney Skolsky that all she wore to bed was Chanel No. 5. Eventually, Fox's Head of Publicity, Harry Brand, instructed his assistant, Roy Craft, to ask Marilyn to tone her behavior down because the studio was supposedly receiving an increasing amount of written complaints from the PTA and various church groups. This she agreed to do, before, of course, continuing as usual.

She also injected her on-screen song, "Kiss," with a subtle eroticism. When it was announced that this was to be released as a single record, cocomposer Lionel Newman suggested that MM's lips be imprinted on the disc. The record company, MGM, did not want to stir up more controversy, however. "In those days they didn't take such chances," Newman later said. "But Marilyn was willing to do it. She thought it was great."

Top: *Marilyn costume-tests a Dorothy Jeakins outfit that was rejected for the movie.* Bottom: *Here she models the costume that helped her wiggle her way to stardom.*

Far left: *Marilyn captured the essence of her character by carefully studying her script.* Left: *But her famous walk was something that basically came naturally to her.*

JEAN PETERS

Jean Peters got the role of Polly Cutler in Niagara *only after Anne Baxter pulled out of the movie, aware that it was being reworked to spotlight the talents of Marilyn Monroe. After* As Young As You Feel *and* O. Henry's Full House, *this was the third and last project on which Jean and Marilyn worked together.*

Born Elizabeth Jean Peters in Canton, Ohio, on October 15, 1926, the wholesome brunette won a trip to Hollywood in 1946 as a prize for taking the title of Miss Ohio State. In 1947, she made her screen debut with Tyrone Power in Captain from Castile.

Top left: *Marilyn simmers on-screen as she shares a passionate moment with Richard Allen.* Bottom left: *Her sizzle was due in part to Henry Hathaway, who said, "She's the best natural actress I've directed."*

CREDITS

Twentieth Century-Fox

Produced by Sol C. Siegel

Directed by Howard Hawks

Screenplay by Charles Lederer

Based on the musical comedy by
Anita Loos and Joseph Fields

Photographed in Technicolor by
Harry J. Wild

Art direction by Lyle Wheeler and
Joseph C. Wright

Music by Lionel Newman

Choreographed by Jack Cole

Released August 1953

SONGS BY MM

"Two Little Girls from Little
Rock" (with Jane Russell)

"When Love Goes Wrong"
(with Jane Russell)

"Bye Bye Baby"

"Diamonds Are a Girl's
Best Friend"

*"Square-cut or pear-shaped, these rocks don't lose their shape." Marilyn's unforgettable rendition of
"Diamonds Are a Girl's Best Friend" remains her most enduring screen performance.*

THE FILMS OF MARILYN MONROE

GENTLEMEN PREFER BLONDES

Gus Esmond's plans to marry Lorelei Lee, a scorching blonde bombshell with a fondness for money, are thwarted by his cynical millionaire father. The young couple then agree to meet and marry in Paris after Lorelei has traveled there aboard the *Ile de France* with her showgirl friend, Dorothy. Dorothy is to act as chaperon to keep men away from Lorelei and vice versa. Esmond, Sr., meanwhile, resolves to turn his son against Lorelei by hiring a private detective named Malone to gather incriminating evidence against her during the trip. The detective complies by taking an incriminating photo of a flirtatious, elderly diamond magnate, Sir Francis "Beeky" Beekman, attempting to demonstrate on Lorelei how a python squeezes a goat! Dorothy, who is attracted to Malone but upset by his job, helps Lorelei retrieve the photo, which could get Lorelei and Beeky in trouble with Gus and Mrs. Beekman. In return for helping him out of a potentially sticky situation, Beeky reluctantly gives Lady Beekman's diamond tiara to Lorelei. Upon arriving in Paris, Lorelei and Dorothy discover that Gus has withdrawn their letter of credit, forcing them to seek work in a nightclub. Still love struck, Gus tracks the pair down at the Paris nightclub just as Lorelei is about to be arrested for stealing Lady Beekman's tiara. Lorelei then discovers that the tiara has disappeared, making it look as though she is truly guilty. The case is dropped after Malone figures out that Beekman is the thief and forces the old man to tell the truth in court. All ends well with Lorelei and Dorothy pairing up with Gus and Malone for a double wedding ceremony.

BEHIND THE SCENES

Originally a 1928 film with Ruth Taylor and Alice White, and then a smash Broadway musical starring Carol Channing, *Gentlemen Prefer Blondes* was purchased for $500,000 by Twentieth Century-Fox in 1952 as a vehicle for Betty Grable. Shortly thereafter, previews of *Niagara* confirmed that the studio possessed a much more potent and a far less expensive sex symbol than Grable. The former "Pin-Up Girl" was earning $150,000

The costars' physical similarities were considerably less than this poster implied.

"A kiss on the hand might feel very good, but a diamond tiara lasts forever!"

per picture in the early 1950s while Marilyn was making a contracted maximum of $1,500 per week.

Thus, Marilyn Monroe was cast in the role of Lorelei Lee. The shooting commenced in November 1952, and the film was completed three months later. Upon release the following summer, many people had good reason to feel happy: the moviegoers, who flocked to see this major musical of the era; Marilyn, who was now an international superstar; and the Fox executives, who had paid just $18,000 for its hottest star to appear in this role.

One person who was less than delighted about the whole experience, however, was legendary director Howard Hawks. Hawks had been antagonized not only by Marilyn's customary lateness to the set but also her insistence on reshooting scenes that he had already approved. The gruff director had been satisfied, for instance, with the first take of the "Bye Bye Baby" production number, but MM demanded another ten. Time is money in feature-film production, and Marilyn was costing the studio plenty with her demand for retakes. When the Fox front office asked how production could be sped up, Hawkes retorted, ". . . three wonderful ideas: Replace Marilyn, rewrite the script and make it shorter, and get a new director."

Three musical sequences were eventually cut from the finished film—"Four French Dances," "Down Boy," and "When the Wild Wild Women Go Swimmin' Down in the Bimini Bay." Fortunately, Marilyn's signature performance of "Diamonds Are a Girl's Best Friend" remained intact. The number confirmed Darryl F. Zanuck's prediction that, "If anyone has doubts as to the future of Marilyn Monroe, *Gentlemen Prefer Blondes* is the answer."

Despite appearances, the studio was earning the fortune, not its brightest star.

The "Two Little Girls from Little Rock" depend on their large talents to woo the audience.

The girls admit, "When love goes wrong, nothing goes right."

GRAUMAN'S CHINESE THEATER

This legendary Hollywood Boulevard venue, which boasts a cement forecourt decorated with the signatures, handprints, and footprints of many of the world's top movie stars, invited the two female stars of Gentlemen Prefer Blondes *to add their own contributions on June 26, 1953. Marilyn initially suggested that her bust and Jane Russell's bottom—the actresses' most celebrated assets—should be imprinted in cement for posterity, but Grauman's was not amused. She settled for the more conventional hand- and footprints, plus a rhinestone (instead of a diamond) to dot the "i" in her signature.*

Top left: *Lorelei (MM) uses her persuasive charms to secure Gus Esmond's (Tommy Noonan) support.* Bottom left: *While Dorothy utilizes some of her own charm to hook Malone (Elliott Reid).*

CAST

Pola Debevoise . .Marilyn Monroe
Loco Dempsey . . .Betty Grable
Schatze Page. . . .Lauren Bacall
Freddie Denmark . .David Wayne
Eben . . . . .Rory Calhoun
Tom Brookman . . . .
. . . . . . .Cameron Mitchell
J. Stewart Merrill . .Alex D'Arcy
Waldo Brewster. . . .Fred Clark
J.D. Hanley . . .William Powell
Mike, Elevator Man . . . . . .
. . . . .George Dunn
Benton . . . . .Percy Helton
Cab Driver . . .Robert Adler
Elevator Operator . .Harry Carter
Mr. Otis . . . . . .Tudor Owen
Antoine . . . .Maurice Marsac
Man at Bridge . .Emmett Vogan
Madame . . . .Hermine Sterler
Secretary . . . . .Abney Mott
Bennett . . . .Rankin Mansfield
Tony. . . . . . . .Jan Arvan
Captain of Waiters . . . . . .
. . . . . . .Ivan Triesault

CREDITS

Twentieth Century-Fox

Produced and written by
Nunnally Johnson

Directed by Jean Negulesco

Based on plays by Zoe Akins,
Dale Eunson, and Katherine Albert

Photographed in CinemaScope
and Technicolor by
Joe MacDonald

Art direction by Lyle Wheeler and
Leland Fuller

Musical direction by
Alfred Newman

Incidental music by
Cyril Mockridge

Released November 1953

*Marilyn, on top of the world as an actress, was about to marry Joe DiMaggio. But behind the smile,
there was a confused, insecure woman seeking solace in pills and alcohol.*

THE FILMS OF MARILYN MONROE

HOW TO MARRY
A MILLIONAIRE

Hoping to lure millionaire marrying material their way, department store models Pola, Schatze, and Loco rent an expensive New York apartment. Initially unsuccessful at their scheme, the young women find their luck is about to change. Having mistakenly rejected the advances of millionaire Tom Brookman, believing him to be a mere garage hand, Schatze sets her sights on a middle-aged oil tycoon named J.D. Hanley. Loco travels to Maine with her wealthy magnate, Waldo Brewster, only to discover that the "lodge" he is taking her to is not the Elks' Lodge Convention, but his private hunting lodge. Her return to New York is delayed by a bout of measles, but in the meantime, she meets and falls in love with a forest ranger named Eben. Pola is supposed to rendezvous with wealthy J. Stewart Merrill in Atlantic City, but because she is too vain to wear her glasses in public, she boards the wrong plane. On board, she meets and falls for Freddie Denmark, the owner of the girls' apartment, who is en route to sort out a dispute with the Internal Revenue Service. Freddie eventually resolves the problem, but only after a fight with his accountant lands him in a neck brace. Loco and Pola return to New York with Eben and Freddie—their new husbands—while Hanley convinces Schatze that she would be happier with Tom Brookman because love is more important than money. When Tom pulls out a huge wad of cash to pay the check at the local diner, Schatze discovers she has both.

A remake of the vintage 1932 comedy *The Greeks Had a Word For Them*, *How to Marry a Millionaire* enabled Marilyn to once again display her talents as a deadpan comedienne. Yet, supposedly, she was as reluctant as her on-screen character to appear in glasses, because she was concerned that this might diminish her sex appeal. According to director Jean Negulesco, he wisely advised her otherwise. "Marilyn, don't try to sell this sex," he told her. "You are sex. You are the institution of sex. The only moti-

MM, William Powell, and Lauren Bacall on a lobby card promoting CinemaScope's advantage over 3-D movies.

Director Jean Negulesco feasts his eyes on the incoming and outgoing queens of Twentieth Century-Fox.

vation you need for this part is the fact that in the movie you are as blind as a bat without glasses."

Negulesco, who had a reputation as a woman's director, got along well with Marilyn, even painting her portrait at one point and loaning her several books. Unlike later directors Marilyn worked with, he understood and accepted her insecurities.

Yet, time and again, those working with her on the set saw these insecurities surface and panic set in. During one scene, in which Marilyn's character was to receive a telephone call, Marilyn became confused to the point of answering the phone before it rang; in another scene, in which she was to drink coffee, she tried to drink out of the cup before she filled it.

Lauren Bacall had mixed feelings toward Marilyn, stemming from MM's habitual tardiness and her constant need for retakes. Bacall felt pressured by having to be at the top of her form for every one of the 15 or more takes that Marilyn sometimes insisted on. Marilyn tended to get better and better as she became more familiar and secure with a scene, while her costars often lost their edge and their spontaneity. Bacall nonetheless liked Marilyn, and in her autobiography, she recalled an occasion when MM tried to strike up a conversation with her young son, Steve. Bacall writes that Marilyn asked the boy, "'How old are you?' He said, 'I'm four.' She: 'But you're so big for four. I would have thought you were two or three.' He wasn't, and was confused (so was I, so was she). . . .'"

Pola (MM) is amazed to see how much J.D. (William Powell) is spoiling Schatze (Lauren Bacall).

Neither Travilla's exotic costume nor Marilyn's intriguing pose were used on-screen.

Schatze (Lauren Bacall), Tom (Cameron Mitchell), and Pola (MM) share a burger and a surprise in the film's closing scene.

BETTY GRABLE

A top-ten box office star for a record 13 years, Betty Grable (1916-1973) was the actress whom Marilyn admired, imitated, and eventually replaced as queen of the Fox lot. Resenting Fox's hand in the decline of her popularity, Grable tore up her contract with the studio during the production of How to Marry a Millionaire *and consequently relinquished her top-billing (to guess who?). Yet she bore no animosity toward Marilyn. After Grable's departure, MM moved into her dressing room at Fox but never really filled the niche Grable carved out in American pop culture. No one has.*

Top left: *In Monroe, Grable, and Bacall, the film had a triple-engined box-office draw.* Bottom left: *Marilyn gave an endearing and accomplished comic performance in the film.*

RIVER OF NO RETURN

The film provided overtime pay for the sound and camera crews and time off for the scriptwriter.

Kay (MM) struggles to free herself from Matt's (Robert Mitchum) grip as their burning passion intensifies.

STORYLINE

Matt Calder is released from jail after serving a sentence for shooting a man in the back in order to save a friend. With his son, Mark, he plans to work his small farm, which borders on the River of No Return. One morning, Matt and Mark rescue Kay and Harry Weston from an out-of-control raft. When Matt warns them that any journey by river is impossible, Harry runs off with Matt's gun and horse. Matt, Mark, and Kay are forced to escape marauding Indians by taking the raft down the treacherous river. Matt vows to avenge Harry for his misdeed. Kay desperately tries to persuade him otherwise, and, in a fit of temper, she tells Matt that she knows about his past. Mark overhears the argument and refuses to believe his father's explanation of the crime. Despite the disagreements, Kay and Matt fall in love. The group reach Council City, where Kay finds Harry and begs him to apologize to Matt. Harry agrees, but when he sees the unarmed Calder, he pulls out his gun. Mark saves his father by shooting Harry in the back; the boy then understands his father's past actions.

BEHIND THE SCENES

Shot in the Canadian Rockies, *River of No Return* ran over schedule and over budget. Part of the problem was director Otto Preminger, who insisted that the scenes of the raft struggling down the rapids be filmed with real actors, as opposed to stuntmen, resulting in a series of mishaps that delayed shooting. On one occasion, Marilyn had to be saved from drowning when she fell into the river and her boots filled with water. On another, she and Mitchum had to be rescued when the raft became stuck on a rock and was on the verge of turning over. Next, Marilyn sprained her ankle and began hobbling around the set on crutches. Joe DiMaggio rushed to the location with his own personal doctor, but Marilyn's friend, actress Shelley Winters, later claimed in her autobiography that it was all a ruse. Marilyn was trying to get back at Preminger because the two had clashed over the presence of Natasha Lytess on the set.

Top: *MM described* River *as "a grade 'Z' cowboy movie, in which the acting finishes third to the scenery and CinemaScope." Bottom: She feigned injury as revenge on director Otto Preminger.*

THE FILMS OF MARILYN MONROE

THERE'S NO BUSINESS LIKE SHOW BUSINESS

Glamour, songs, and the bonus of seeing Johnnie Ray become a priest!

MM donned some of Travilla's most stunning creations for her role in this glittery movie.

STORYLINE

The Five Donahues, a vaudeville act featuring Molly and Terry Donahue and their children, Steve, Katy, and Tim, turns into the Four Donahues after Steve quits to join the priesthood. Tim falls in love with Vicky, an ambitious singer, and soon the family act disintegrates completely. Tim and Katy agree to join Vicky in her forthcoming Broadway show. Tim is unable to control his feelings for Vicky and accuses her of having an affair with the producer, Lew Harris. On opening night, Tim gets drunk, smashes up a car, and disappears after his father reprimands him for his unprofessional behavior. Molly takes Tim's place in the show and is a great success, but she blames Vicky for her son's problems. An inconsolable Terry gives up stage work to look for Tim. It is only when Katy takes charge that the situation is resolved. Backstage at a benefit show, Katy finally brings Molly and Vicky together. When Molly takes the stage, Steve, now an army chaplain, turns up in the wings, as does Tim who has enlisted in the navy. Terry follows, and soon the Five Donahues are reunited.

BEHIND THE SCENES

On January 14, 1954, Marilyn married Joe DiMaggio, which affected her career in ways that she could never have predicted. Fox had promised to feature MM in the screen version of the hit Broadway comedy *The Seven Year Itch* if Marilyn agreed to first boost the box-office potential of *There's No Business Like Show Business*. The part of Vicky was created especially for this purpose, and numbers such as "Heat Wave"—originally intended for the Molly Donahue character—were assigned to MM's character. Ethel Merman would have probably delivered "Heat Wave" in her characteristic barnstorming manner, but Marilyn flavored the song in her own style— one rife with erotic overtones. DiMaggio was less than delighted with his wife's exhibitionism, and his pressure tactics began to get to Marilyn. On one occasion, MM confided to dress designer Billy Travilla that she felt as if she was losing her mind. "I don't want to be seen this way," she told him. "If I go crazy, please take me away and hide me."

CAST

Molly Donahue . .Ethel Merman
Tim Donahue .Donald O'Connor
Vicky . . . . .Marilyn Monroe
Terrance Donahue . .Dan Dailey
Steve Donahue . . .Johnnie Ray
Katy Donahue . . .Mitzi Gaynor
Lew Harris . . .Richard Eastham
Charles Gibbs. . .Hugh O'Brian
Eddie Duggan . .Frank McHugh
Father Dineen. . .Rhys Williams
Marge . . . . . .Lee Patrick
Helen (Hat Check Girl). . . .
. . . . .Eve Miller
Lillian Sawyer . .Robin Raymond
Katy's Boyfriend . . .Alvy Moore
Stage Manager . . .Lyle Talbot
Harry. . . . . .Chick Chandler

CREDITS

Twentieth Century-Fox
Produced by Sol C. Siegel
Directed by Walter Lang
Screenplay by Phoebe and
Henry Ephron
From a story by Lamar Trotti
Photographed in Deluxe Color and
CinemaScope by Leon Shamroy
Art Direction by Lyle Wheeler
and John De Cuir
Music by Alfred Newman and
Lionel Newman
Dances staged by Robert Alton
Released December 1954

SONGS BY MM

"After You Get What You Want
You Don't Want It"
"Heat Wave"
"Lazy" (with Mitzi Gaynor and
Donald O'Connor)
"There's No Business Like Show
Business" (with cast)

Top: *"Heatwave"—one of MM's most suggestive dance routines.* Bottom: *Donald O'Connor and Mitzi Gaynor's energetic dancing was contrasted with MM's sensual singing style in "Lazy."*

THE FILMS OF MARILYN MONROE

CAST

The Girl . . . .Marilyn Monroe
Richard Sherman . . .Tom Ewell
Helen Sherman . . .Evelyn Keyes
Tom MacKenzie . . .Sonny Tufts
Kruhulik . . . . .Robert Strauss
Dr. Brubaker . .Oscar Homolka
Miss Morris. . . . .
. . . . .Marguerite Chapman
Plumber. . . . .Victor Moore
Elaine. . . . . . . .Roxanne
Mr. Brady . . .Donald MacBride
Miss Finch . . . .Carolyn Jones
Ricky Sherman . .Butch Bernard
Waitress . . . .Doro Merande
Girl . . . . . . .Dorothy Ford

CREDITS

Twentieth Century-Fox

Produced by Charles K. Feldman
and Billy Wilder

Directed by Billy Wilder

Screenplay by Billy Wilder and
George Axelrod

Based on the play by George
Axelrod

Photographed in Deluxe Color
and CinemaScope by
Milton Krasner

Art Direction by Lyle Wheeler
and George W. Davis

Music by Alfred Newman

Released June 1955

Looking happy on the Itch *set during a break in filming the closing scene. Shortly afterward,
Marilyn divorced Joe DiMaggio, broke her contract with Fox, and departed for New York.*

THE SEVEN YEAR ITCH

Middle-aged publishing executive Richard Sherman remains behind in Manhattan while his wife, Helen, and son, Ricky, depart for their summer vacation. He resolves not to behave like the thousands of other New York husbands in his situation. He will not overindulge in food, drink, or women. But, Sherman possesses a colorful imagination, and he allows his thoughts to run wild when he encounters the beautiful model who has just sublet the apartment upstairs. Her positive response to his invitation to join him for a drink prompts immediate visions of a passionate affair, but when these thoughts spill over into reality, his attempt to kiss her only results in the two of them falling off a piano stool. The uninhibited TV model thinks nothing of the incident. However, Sherman's guilt has him convinced that The Girl is telling all of America that he is a sex fiend and that his wife is seeking consolation in an affair of her own with her novelist friend Tom MacKenzie. Sherman's paranoia increases when he reads a report describing a condition whereby couples grow restless after seven years of marriage. Nevertheless, that evening he invites The Girl to join him for dinner and a movie. Afterward, he reluctantly allows her to stay the night in his apartment, which, unlike hers, has air conditioning. Even though he sleeps in the living room, he imagines himself being black-mailed and Helen returning home to shoot him. When Tom MacKenzie arrives to collect a canoe paddle that little Ricky had left behind, Sherman panics, knocks Tom out, and insists on going to the lake to give his son the paddle himself. The Girl confides that, while Sherman may not be handsome, he is a truly nice man whom she could easily fall in love with. Sherman, his sense of reality restored, permits her to stay in the apartment while he is away.

The Seven Year Itch is the movie that cemented Marilyn's image as the beautiful, sweet-natured goddess of love—a wide-eyed innocent who thinks

MM was the main attraction, but Tom Ewell gave a bravura performance.

Tom Ewell looks down, while the man operating the wind machine underneath the grating looks up.

that everything is "just elegant," recognizes classical music "because there's no vocal," and stays cool by storing her panties in the refrigerator. "Marilyn Monroe doesn't just play The Girl," said the play's author, George Axelrod. "She is The Girl."

Shooting began in Hollywood on August 10, 1954, immediately after Marilyn had completed her work on *There's No Business Like Show Business*. On September 9, the cast and crew flew to New York for the location shots. Five nights later, almost 4,000 people gathered about 2:00 a.m. near the Trans-Lux Theater at 52nd Street and Lexington Avenue to watch the filming of the famous skirt scene, in which The Girl finds relief from the summer heat by standing over a subway grate and allowing the breeze to billow up her skirt.

Standing in the crowd, Joe DiMaggio became incensed at his wife's latest public display, and, this incident reportedly proved to be the last straw in the couple's stormy marriage. They returned to California shortly thereafter, announced their separation in early October, and were divorced at the end of the month.

Following her last day of work on November 5, Marilyn decided to reshape her life, both personally and professionally. Just before Christmas of 1954, she walked out on her Fox contract and, traveling under the name of Zelda Zonk, flew to New York. Marilyn did not return to Hollywood for over a year. When she did return, following the smash success of *The Seven Year Itch*, she did so strictly on her own terms.

MM is dressed up to resemble Mae West for a fantasy sequence that was cut from the film.

Q: "Would you mind fastening my straps in the back?"
A: "Oh, sure . . . sure!"

Photographers and fans snapping photos during this famous scene ruined many takes. Director Billy Wilder promised the fans a special opportunity to take photos later so that filming could continue.

TOM EWELL

Born S. Yewell Tompkins in Owensboro, Kentucky, on April 29, 1909, the former Macy's salesman was an established stage actor by the time he made his screen debut in Adam's Rib. *Ewell's role in* The Seven Year Itch *was a reprise of his standout performance in the 1952 Broadway production. Despite further success opposite Jayne Mansfield in* The Girl Can't Help It, *Hollywood failed to capitalize on his talents. In 1962 he was reduced to singing to a pig in the Pat Boone vehicle* State Fair! *Thereafter, his screen appearances were sporadic. Ewell enjoyed far greater success on the stage.*

Top left: *In Sherman's imagination, The Girl tells a plumber (Victor Moore) about Sherman's lechery.* Bottom left: *In a more optimistic vision, he also imagines her as his femme fatale.*

CAST

Cherie . . . . .Marilyn Monroe
Bo Decker . . . . .Don Murray
Virgil . . . . .Arthur O'Connell
Grace . . . . . . .Betty Field
Vera. . . . . . .Eileen Heckart
Carl . . . . .Robert Bray
Elma . . . . . . .Hope Lange
Life Photographer . . . .
. . . . .Hans Conried
Life Reporter . . .Casey Adams
Nightclub Manager. .Henry Slate
Gerald . . . . . .Terry Kellman
Evelyn . . . . . . .Linda Brace
Cover Girl . . . .Greta Thyssen
Landlady . . . . .Helen Mayon
Blonde on Street . .Lucille Knox
Elderly Passengers . . . .
Kate MacKenna, George Selk

CREDITS

Twentieth Century-Fox

Produced by Buddy Adler

Directed by Joshua Logan

Screenplay by George Axelrod

Based on the play by
William Inge

Photographed in Eastman Color
and CinemaScope by
Milton Krasner

Art Direction by Lyle Wheeler
and Mark-Lee Kirk

Music by Alfred Newman and
Cyril Mockridge

Released August 1956

SONGS BY MM

"That Old Black Magic"

Armed with Method acting techniques, her own production company, and a vastly improved Fox contract, Marilyn enjoys her new-found power back in Hollywood on the set of Bus Stop.

BUS STOP

Cherie, a less-than-talented singer at the Blue Dragon Cafe in Phoenix, Arizona, is initially flattered by the attention heaped on her by handsome young Montana cowboy, Bo Decker. But she soon becomes confused by his wild, headstrong behavior and frightened by his impulsive decision to marry her. Bo, accompanied by his mature, wisened friend Virgil, is in town to participate in the rodeo. Cherie, who is annoyed by the younger man's habit of pronouncing her name "Cherry," quickly discovers that there are major differences in their personalities and lifestyles. Whereas Bo is naive about love and sex because he has spent most of his life isolated on a ranch, Cherie has had many boyfriends, lovers, and companions. She has steadily been making her way west to Hollywood since she left the Ozarks, hoping for a career in the movies. Virgil understands that the two are mismatched despite Bo's ardor, and he slips Cherie the money to escape to Los Angeles. Bo finds out and forces her to join him and Virgil on the bus back to Montana. When the bus stops at Grace's Diner for a break, Cherie and Elma, a fellow passenger, sneak inside while Bo is still asleep to notify others about the kidnapping. Bo wakes up to find Cherie's suitcase is gone. His chauvinistic attempt to carry his reluctant sweetheart out of the diner and to a nearby minister is thwarted by Carl, the bus driver, who defeats Bo in a fair fistfight. The next morning, Virgil persuades Bo to make his apologies to everyone for his ungentlemanly behavior. In a tender moment, Cherie informs her humbled admirer that she is not as innocent as he imagined her to be. But this matters little to Bo, who responds with a renewed offer of marriage based on mutual respect and consideration. The happy couple can now continue their journey to Montana, while Virgil decides to stay behind as his young companion no longer needs him.

BEHIND THE SCENES

In the months between *The Seven Year Itch* and *Bus Stop*, Marilyn had trained in the style of acting known as the Method, discarded coach

Published by Bantam in 1956, the book based on the film is now a collectors' item.

MM's hair was dyed reddish blonde for her role as the romantically confused Cherie.

Elma (Hope Lange) helps placate the abducted Cherie (MM) when their bus stops at a roadside diner.

Bo (Don Murray) insists that Cherie (MM) leave with him, but his plans are disrupted.

Natasha Lytess in favor of Paula Strasberg, established her own production company with photographer Milton Greene, and secured a lucrative contract with Twentieth Century-Fox that gave her storyline, director, and cinematographer approval. When Marilyn returned to Hollywood in February of 1956, it was at the peak of her career and the top of her form. Her performance as Cherie is generally considered her best.

A Broadway hit the previous year, *Bus Stop* (also titled *The Wrong Kind of Girl* for some prints) began shooting in May of 1956. While her recent training benefitted her performance, Marilyn's new-found power brought with it an uncharacteristic arrogance that caused friction on the set. Prime targets were Don Murray and Hope Lange, who were not only making their screen debuts but were also involved in a romance that led to marriage that same year. (They divorced in 1961.)

Marilyn objected to the color of Lange's hair, claiming that it was too fair and detracted from her own. The result was that the newcomer's hair was dyed a darker shade. Murray, a graduate of the American Academy of Dramatic Arts, was subjected to Marilyn's derision because of his inexperience in making movies. He suffered painful facial cuts when the star overdid a scene in which she had to slap him with the sequined tail of her costume. Director Joshua Logan begged her to apologize, but, for reasons known only to herself, she refused.

When the film was released, Marilyn's tender, well-balanced performance as the Southern-accented Cherie was praised by the critics, particularly by Bosley Crowther of *The New York Times*, who had been unimpressed with Marilyn up to that point. Crowther began his review, "Hold onto your chairs, everybody, and get set for a rattling surprise. Marilyn Monroe has finally proved herself an actress in *Bus Stop*. . . . If you don't find Miss M. a downright Duce, you'll find her a dilly, anyhow."

JOSHUA LOGAN

Logan was not only the director of such movies as Mister Roberts *and* Picnic, *he was also a playwright and a stage director. He was selected by Marilyn for* Bus Stop *because he had studied a method-style acting under Konstantin Stanislavski at the Moscow Art Theatre during the 1930s.*

Sometimes driven to distraction by Marilyn's lateness, Logan still managed to champion Marilyn's talents. He later revealed, "I finally realized that I had a chance of working with the greatest artist I'd ever worked with in my life, and it was Marilyn Monroe. I couldn't believe it."

Top left: *Marilyn's beautifully rendered facial expressions and Southern accent perfectly captured the character of Cherie.* Bottom left: *She was expertly supported by both Don Murray and Arthur O'Connell.*

CAST

Grand Duke Charles . . . . . .
. . . . . . .Laurence Olivier
Elsie Marina. . .Marilyn Monroe
Queen Dowager . . . .
. . . . .Sybil Thorndike
King Nicholas . .Jeremy Spenser
Northbrook . . .Richard Wattis
Maisie Springfield . . .Jean Kent
Colonel Hoffman. . . . . . .
. . . . .Esmond Knight
Fanny. . . . .Daphne Anderson
Betty. . . . . . . .Vera Day
Major Domo . . .Paul Hardwick
Valet with Violin. . . . . . .
. . . . . .Andrea Malandrinos
Lottie. . . . . .Margot Lister
Maud . . .Rosamund Greenwood
The Ambassador. . . . . . .
. . . . . . .Aubrey Dexter
Lady Sunningdale . . . . . .
. . . . . . .Maxine Audley
Call Boy . . . .Harold Goodwin
Maggie . . . . .Gillian Owen

CREDITS

A Warner Bros. Presentation
of a Film by
Marilyn Monroe Productions, Inc.
and L.O.P. Ltd.

Executive Producer
Milton H. Greene

Produced and directed by
Laurence Olivier

Screenplay by Terence Rattigan

Based on Rattigan's play
The Sleeping Prince

Photographed in Technicolor by
Jack Cardiff

Art Direction by Carmen Dillon

Music by Richard Addinsell

Dances arranged by
William Chappell

Released July 1957

*An alluring 1950s-style publicity shot, which, oddly enough, was conceived to promote a period film
featuring MM in Beatrice Dawson-designed costumes dating from about 1911.*

THE PRINCE AND THE SHOWGIRL

STORYLINE

Among the distinguished visitors to London for the 1911 coronation of George V is Grand Duke Charles, Prince Regent of Carpathia. Accompanying the Grand Duke is his son King Nicholas and his mother-in-law, the Queen Dowager. Eager to please the Grand Duke in order to secure a peaceful relationship with Carpathia, the British Foreign Office smoothes the way for him to invite American chorus girl Elsie Marina to the Carpathian Embassy. Yet, Elsie is not overly impressed with the Regent's approach to romance. After rebuffing his advances all evening, she adds insult to injury by drinking too much and falling asleep. He, of course, is furious and wants nothing more to do with her, but when she awakes in the Embassy the next morning Elsie realizes that she is in love. Against the Regent's wishes, the Queen Dowager commands Elsie to accompany them to the Abbey as her Lady-in-Waiting, and Nicholas later invites her to the Coronation Ball. The Regent's son has been plotting to overthrow his father and prematurely assume the throne, but Elsie manages to reconcile the two men and in the process regains the admiration of Carpathia's leader. The Regent announces that he is returning to his country, but will come back for Elsie when Nicholas is old enough to succeed him in 18 months time. She agrees to wait, and in the meantime goes back to the musical show, *The Coconut Girl*.

This lobby card showing modern attire was aimed at countering public aversion to historical comedies.

BEHIND THE SCENES

When Marilyn landed at London Airport on July 14, 1956, with two dozen pieces of luggage, new husband Arthur Miller, business partner Milton Greene and his wife, Amy, acting coach Paula Strasberg, and friend-cum-secretary Hedda Rosten, the British press and public were ready to greet her with open arms. But, by the time she departed for the States on November 20, Marilyn's distant, unpleasant attitude had alienated many of the people who had initially welcomed her, a situation that paralleled her association with director/costar Laurence Olivier.

Grand Duke Charles (Olivier) vainly attempts to woo Elsie (MM) with his overtly regal charms.

Their association began pleasantly enough: He called her "Sweetie," and she addressed him as "Larry." Shortly thereafter, Sweetie's frequent habit of arriving to the set hours late—or not at all—infuriated Larry. Olivier himself did little to win her affection and loyalty when he tactfully suggested that she brighten her "yellowish" teeth by brushing them with lemon and baking soda!

Grand Duke Charles is not amused when Elsie returns his advances by falling asleep.

Olivier was further antagonized by the presence of Paula Strasberg on the set as well as Marilyn's constant need for inspiration to fuel her Method acting techniques. On one occasion, he suggested that instead of searching for "the right motivation," she should simply sit still, count to three, and then speak. When this failed to work, he shouted, "Can't you count either?"

Just after the announcement that Olivier was teaming with Monroe for a screen version of Terrence Rattigan's play *The Sleeping Prince*, Joshua Logan had warned him not to "order her about, because it'll throw her and you won't get anything out of her." Olivier later complained, "You never told me what to do when I'm explaining a scene to her and she walks away from me in midsentence."

Larry lights Sweetie's cigarette at the February 1956 press conference held to announce their joint project.

Nevertheless, Marilyn's polished performance in the finished film was sufficient to earn her Italy's David di Donatello Prize and France's Crystal Star Award for Best Foreign Actress, while in his memoirs Olivier wryly observed that people thought, "I was as good as could be, and Marilyn! Marilyn was quite wonderful, the best of all. So. What do you know?"

Marilyn's character, Elsie, was an American chorus girl. As such, Milton Greene wanted MM to sing in the film, but Arthur Miller rejected the idea.

Photo by Milton Green.

MILTON GREENE

Milton Hawthorne Greene the noted photographer with whom Marilyn formed her own production company in 1954, negotiated her ground-breaking contract with Fox. He also helped Marilyn choose her films and directors. On Bus Stop *and* The Prince and the Showgirl, *he designed her makeup and helped design the lighting. But during the production of* Showgirl, *Greene's friendliness toward Olivier was resented by Marilyn, and he repeatedly clashed with Arthur Miller over matters of artistic control. Shortly after filming was completed, Greene sold his shares in Marilyn Monroe Productions, Inc.*

Warner Bros.' marketing tactics for the movie are fairly clear when comparing MM's actual on-screen appearance (top left) with this inappropriate lobby card photo (bottom left).

CREDITS

A United Artists Release

A Mirisch Company Presentation
of an Ashton Picture

Produced and directed by
Billy Wilder

Screenplay by Billy Wilder and
I.A.L. Diamond

Suggested by a story by
R. Thoeren and M. Logan

Photographed by Charles Lang, Jr.

Art Direction by Ted Haworth

Music by Adolph Deutsch

Released March 1959

SONGS BY MM

"Running Wild"

"I Wanna Be Loved by You"

"I'm Through with Love"

*Sugar (MM) and Junior (Tony Curtis): The ukulele-playing singer with a penchant for sax players
and men who wear glasses unwittingly finds her ideal in the musician-cum-playboy.*

SOME LIKE IT HOT

STORYLINE

Joe and Jerry, two struggling musicians, happen to witness the 1929 St. Valentine's Day Massacre. As they flee the scene, they are spotted by the men who arranged this notorious holiday event, Spats Colombo and his gang. Realizing that they must leave Chicago immediately, Joe and Jerry don dresses and wigs, join an all-female jazz orchestra, and board a train for Florida. During the trip, Joe (now Josephine) and Jerry (now Daphne) befriend Sugar, a singer and ukulele player with a fondness for bootleg liquor and a burning desire to marry a millionaire. Both Joe and Jerry fall for Sugar, but when they arrive in Florida, it is Joe who hatches a scheme to woo her by posing as Junior, the suave heir to the Shell Oil fortune. He invites Sugar for drinks aboard a yacht that actually belongs to Osgood Fielding III, a wealthy philanderer who is crazy about Daphne/Jerry. Sugar hopes to marry "Junior," while Daphne/Jerry seriously considers marrying Osgood for the security it would bring! All plans are thrown into disarray when Spats and his men arrive at their hotel for a gangster convention. Joe and Jerry are spotted, but during the mayhem that follows, Spats is murdered by a rival gang. Josephine and Daphne then escape on Osgood's speedboat with their respective partners in tow. Joe has already revealed his true identity to Sugar and is delighted to discover that she accepts him the way he is. And, after removing his wig, Jerry is amazed when he gets a similar response from Osgood!

BEHIND THE SCENES

Some Like It Hot may have been the most successful movie of Marilyn's career, but this famous comedy was made under the least amicable of circumstances. The skill and patience of most of Marilyn's coworkers concealed the problems that plagued production, most of which were caused by her deteriorating mental condition, which was exacerbated by her intake of drugs and alcohol. Marilyn's behavior was generally unreliable and unprofessional for the duration of the shoot.

The movie's musical soundtrack album.

Jerry/Daphne follows his male instincts, rather than Joe's advice, and allows Sugar into his compartment.

*News of her pregnancy made
Marilyn more personally happy
and professionally difficult.*

*MM took another dumb blonde
role to pay Arthur Miller's legal
fees stemming from accusations by
HUAC that he was a pro-communist.*

Sweating under the studio lights in heavy makeup and clothing, stars Jack Lemmon and Tony Curtis often waited hours on the set for Marilyn. If and when she arrived, she had to struggle to remember her dialogue. An oft-told anecdote concerns a scene that required her to simply knock on a door and say, "It's me, Sugar." Supposedly, it took 47 takes to perfect. "After take 30, I had the line put on a blackboard," recalled director Billy Wilder. "She would say things like, 'It's Sugar, me.' "

Another famous story about her inability to perform involves the scene in which Sugar enters Josephine and Daphne's bedroom, rummages through some drawers, and says, "Where's that bourbon?" After 40 takes of Marilyn saying, "Where's the whiskey?," "Where's the bonbon?," or "Where's the bottle?," Wilder pasted the correct line in one of the drawers. He then had to resort to pasting it in every drawer because she became confused as to where he had put it. Reportedly, 59 takes were needed to complete that specific shot. To be fair, there were times when Marilyn did perform well. Those sequences shot on the beach outside the Hotel del Coronado, for example, were done in one or two takes.

A clause in Marilyn's contract stipulated that all her films be in color, but Wilder convinced her that *Some Like It Hot* had to be in black and white because costume tests revealed that Curtis and Lemmon's makeup gave their faces a green tinge. Still, she was concerned—and rightly so—that the two male stars had bigger, more broadly comic roles than she did. She requested that Wilder and cowriter I.A.L. Diamond add some comic bits to the role of Sugar Kane, lest Sugar be just the object of the male characters' attention. Wilder expanded the opening sequence in which the characters board the train to Florida by inserting a scene of Marilyn wobbling across the platform in high heels and then skipping past a puff of steam that blasts across her bottom.

Despite the changes, Marilyn, newly pregnant, was both difficult and uncharacteristically abusive on the set. Wilder, a caustic and cynical man, later summed up the situation by saying, "I knew we were in midflight, and there was a nut on the plane."

TONY CURTIS

Born Bernard Schwartz in the Bronx, Curtis—the star of such diverse films as The Defiant Ones *and* The Boston Strangler *—had a miserable time working with Marilyn. One scene required Curtis to nibble on a chicken leg over and over again because it took 42 takes before Marilyn got her lines correct. He tended to be freshest in the earlier takes, while Marilyn's performance got better in retake after retake. One oft-shot scene in which the couple smooched prompted Curtis to grumble that kissing Marilyn was "like kissing Hitler." Curtis later expressed regret over his remark, claiming that he did not realize how ill Marilyn was.*

Top left: *Tony Curtis enjoys MM's company on the Coronado Beach, California, location that doubled for Miami.* Bottom left: *But, sometimes he spent hours in drag waiting for her arrival.*

A lengthy sequence featuring MM's rendition of the Cole Porter classic "My Heart Belongs to Daddy" helps brighten up what is otherwise Marilyn's weakest starring vehicle.

LET'S MAKE LOVE

French-American billionaire Jean-Marc Clement is dismayed when he learns that he is to be satirized in a forthcoming Broadway revue. Persuaded by his publicity man, Alexander Coffman, to drop in on a rehearsal before taking any action, he visits the small theater and immediately falls for the show's sexy star, Amanda Dell. Mistaken for an actor, Clement agrees to play the part in the show that is a caricature of himself, though no one realizes his true identity. The wealthy playboy not only wants to get close to the object of his desires, he wants to be loved for himself, not his money. He soon learns, however, that Amanda is unimpressed with wealthy men such as Clement. She is also the girlfriend of the show's song-and-dance man, Tony Danton. In order to compete with his unwitting rival in love, the billionaire secretly pays top money for lessons in comedy, singing, and dancing from Milton Berle, Bing Crosby, and Gene Kelly. Furthermore, with financial adviser John Wales acting as the front man, he buys a controlling interest in the revue and eventually replaces Danton as the male lead. Amanda is upset by Danton's firing, but when Clement realizes that her feelings for the singer are those of sympathy, not love, he admits his real identity and proposes marriage. Assuming he is lying, she refuses. As head of Clement Enterprises and owner of the theater, Jean-Marc brings an injunction to close the show down. When Amanda marches to his office to talk the tycoon out of stopping the show, the staff's recognition of Clement convinces her of his real identity.

B E H I N D   T H E   S C E N E S

Obliged to deliver four movies in seven years under her 1955 Twentieth Century-Fox contract, Marilyn had made only *Bus Stop* for the studio by 1959. In the early part of that year, she agreed to star in Fox's *Let's Make Love*. She asked husband Arthur Miller to revise Norman Krasna's screenplay so that greater emphasis was given to the character she was to portray. Miller, in the middle of writing the script for his wife's next vehicle, *The*

A prerelease magazine article aims to introduce Yves Montand to a wider American audience.

Happy with Arthur Miller on the set, Marilyn doomed their marriage while he was away.

Misfits, remained uncredited for his endeavors. Gregory Peck, who had been cast opposite Marilyn, was unhappy with the way his role had been diminished and quit the project.

Peck thought that the Krasna-Miller script was "now about as funny as pushing Grandma down the stairs in a wheelchair." He was not alone in that opinion, for Cary Grant, Charlton Heston, Rock Hudson, James Stewart, and Yul Brynner all turned down the male lead. Eventually Yves Montand, who had starred in the French film version of Miller's play, *The Crucible*, was recruited to play Jean-Marc Clement, a miscasting that was surpassed only by that of the hopelessly wooden Frankie Vaughan in the role of Tony Danton. Apparently, Miller and Marilyn had just seen Montand in a play on Broadway and were impressed enough to suggest him as the male lead.

Let's Make Love was originally titled *The Billionaire* and later retitled *The Millionaire* for French audiences. It is the least successful starring vehicle of Marilyn's career. Its failure represented a sharp turnaround after the triumph of *Some Like It Hot*. At the time of its release, some critics began to view the 34-year-old actress as slightly overweight and, possibly, over-the-hill.

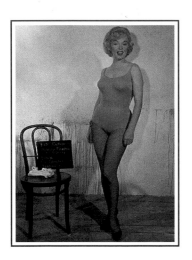

Top: *Wardrobe-testing a costume that appeared in the movie, but a wig that didn't.* Bottom: *Plus, an outfit that emphasized a stunning if slightly fuller hourglass figure.*

Gene Kelly, MM, and Yves Montand relax between scenes. Kelly appeared in a cameo playing himself.

YVES MONTAND

Born Ivo Livi on October 13, 1921, in Monsummano Alto, Italy, Montand was raised in France after his peasant family fled Italy following the rise to power of Mussolini. A nationally famous singer, and star of such movies as The Wages of Fear *(1953) prior to his arrival in Hollywood, his career there was blighted by the headlines stemming from his affair with Marilyn.*

Both married—he to internationally acclaimed actress Simone Signoret—they decided to take the movie's title literally while their respective spouses were away on business, and they were alone in adjoining suites at the Beverly Hills Hilton.

Marilyn likened Montand to a French-speaking Joe DiMaggio and pursued him openly throughout much of 1960, but by the end of the year he made it clear that his future lay in France with his understanding wife. Montand died in 1991.

A final on-screen love scene with Montand concluded an affair that ended less happily in real life.

THE FILMS OF MARILYN MONROE

CAST

Gay Langland . . . .Clark Gable
Roslyn Taber . .Marilyn Monroe
Perce Howland . . . .
. . . . . .Montgomery Clift
Isabelle Steers . . .Thelma Ritter
Guido . . . . . . .Eli Wallach
Old Man in the Bar . . . . .
. . . . .James Barton
Church Lady . .Estelle Winwood
Raymond Taber . . . .
. . . . . . .Kevin McCarthy
Young Boy in Bar . .Dennis Shaw
Charles Steers . .Philip Mitchell
Old Groom . . .Walter Ramage
Fresh Cowboy in Bar . . . . .
. . . . .J. Lewis Smith
Susan. . . . . .Marietta Tree
Bartender. . . .Bobby LaSalle
Man in Bar . . .Ryall Bowker
Ambulance Attendant . . . . .
. . . . .Ralph Roberts

CREDITS

A United Artists Release

A Seven Arts Productions
Presentation of a
John Huston Production

Produced by Frank E. Taylor

Directed by John Huston

Screenplay by Arthur Miller

Photographed by Russell Metty

Art Direction by Stephen Grimes
and William Newberry

Music by Alex North

Released February 1961

The childhood idol: "He never got angry with me once for blowing a line or being late or anything,"
Marilyn recalled about Clark Gable. "He was a gentleman. The best."

THE FILMS OF MARILYN MONROE

THE MISFITS

Divorcée Roslyn Taber and modern-day cowboy Gay Langland immediately fall in love after being introduced by lonesome widower Guido. The two move into Guido's partially completed ranch house, where their different personalities become apparent. Whereas Roslyn is so sensitive as to be fragile, Gay is a self-willed man of action. He stubbornly refuses to listen to her pleas to abort a proposed roundup of some wild horses, which will result in the animals' slaughter and conversion into dog food. Gay's partners in the roundup are Guido and Perce Howland, an alcoholic rodeo rider. All three men share an aversion to "working for wages," that is, working a regular job, which is an infringement on their freedom. Perce eventually succumbs to Roslyn's powers of persuasion and releases the captured mustangs. Gay is furious, and in an attempt to reassert his authority, he risks life and limb to recapture the herd's stallion. Having made his point, he sets the horse free, and, although the venture was not successful, Gay regains Roslyn's love and respect.

As things turned out, The Misfits *was the last completed movie for both Monroe and Gable.*

BEHIND THE SCENES

From the beginning of production until the last frame was shot, *The Misfits* was plagued with monumental problems. Because an actors' strike had caused a five-week delay on *Let's Make Love*, Marilyn had to leave for New York immediately following its completion in order to film three days of costume tests for *The Misfits*. Production had been scheduled to begin March 3, 1960, but delays postponed the start date to mid-July. When Marilyn arrived on location in Reno, Nevada, on July 20, the temperature was averaging an excruciating 110 degrees.

Not the best of working conditions for Marilyn, whose appearance was starting to show the effects of her ongoing problem with insomnia, compounded by a daily diet of Nembutal sleeping pills washed down with either champagne or vodka. On many mornings Allan "Whitey" Snyder had to attend to her makeup while she was still lying in bed. By

Excessive drug and alcohol consumption were beginning to take their toll on the once-soft features.

August 27, Marilyn was so ill she was flown to Westside Hospital in Los Angeles, yet when she returned the following week, she was in such good form that she was able to do a continuous five-minute scene with Montgomery Clift—the longest continuous take of both their careers.

Producer Frank Taylor had alluded to the stellar collection of professionals on both sides of the camera by describing the project as "an attempt at the ultimate motion picture." Yet, after running 40 days over schedule and costing just under $4 million, *The Misfits* became known simply as the most expensive black and white movie made until that time. United Artists executives were unhappy with the rough cut of the film, so John Huston, Arthur Miller, and Frank Taylor agreed to reshoot several scenes. Gable had script approval, however, and he rejected the idea. Other disagreements over the final cut resulted in the elimination of a shot of Marilyn's naked breast from the bedroom scene.

Perhaps the biggest strain involved the final destruction of Marilyn's marriage to Miller. *The Misfits,* which had been expanded from his 1957 short story, had been the playwright's first original screenplay as well as the first major role written especially—and lovingly—for Marilyn. Yet, by the time of production, her infidelity with Yves Montand and Miller's inability to live up to her unreasonable expectations meant that their marriage was virtually over. During filming, they often argued all night in their suite in the Mapes Hotel, and Marilyn would be hostile to Arthur in front of cast and crew, referring to him as "old Grouchy Grumps." Once, she slammed a car door in his face and ordered the driver to leave him behind at a desert location. On November 11, a week after the end of filming, Marilyn announced their official separation.

MM on Montgomery Clift: "He's the only person I know who's in worse shape than I am."

A script conference at the Reno location, with director John Huston (left) and writer Arthur Miller.

Marilyn between scenes with "old Grouchy Grumps."

CLARK GABLE

The legendary star of Gone With the Wind *did not live to see his performance in* The Misfits *or the birth of his only son.*

Bored with waiting for MM to turn up on the set, the 59-year-old Gable opted to do his own stunts, which included being dragged by a truck traveling at 30 mph. On the last day of filming he said, "Christ, I'm glad this picture's finished. She damn near gave me a heart attack." The next day, Gable had a massive heart attack; he died 11 days later. Marilyn was inconsolable at the loss. In May of 1961, she dutifully attended the christening of Gable's only child, John Clark Gable.

Top left: *Superb dramatic acting, opposite the likes of Eli Wallach.* Bottom left: *Posing with Miller (top), Clift (bottom), and (from left) producer Frank Taylor, Wallach, Huston, and Gable.*

Ellen Arden . . .Marilyn Monroe
Nick Arden . . . .Dean Martin
Bianca . . . . . .Cyd Charisse
Steven "Adam" Burkette . . . .
. . . . .Tom Tryon
Shoe Clerk . . . . . .Wally Cox
Insurance Man . . . .Phil Silvers
Dr. Herman Schlick . . . . . .
. . . . .Steve Allen
Tim Arden . . . .
. . .Robert Christopher Morley
Lita Arden . .Alexandra Heilweil
Judge . . . . . .John McGiver
Court Clerk . . . .Grady Sutton
Nick's Secretary . .Elouise Hardt

CREDITS

Twentieth Century-Fox

Produced by Henry T. Weinstein

Directed by George Cukor

Screenplay by Nunnally Johnson
and Walter Bernstein

Based on the screenplay
"My Favorite Wife"
by Bella and Samuel Spewack

From a story by the Spewacks and
Leo McCarey

Photographed by Franz Planer,
Charles Lang, Jr.,
William Daniels, and Leo Tover

Art Direction by Gene Allen

Costumes by Jean-Louis

Filmed April and May 1962

—UNFINISHED—

Marilyn's superb appearance in the nude-swimming scene provides a tantalizing glimpse of what might have been.

THE FILMS OF MARILYN MONROE

SOMETHING'S GOT TO GIVE

STORYLINE

After surviving a plane crash and being marooned on a tropical island for five years, Ellen Arden returns home on the day that a judge has pronounced her officially dead, freeing her husband, Nick, to take Bianca as his new wife. Following Nick and Bianca's departure on their honeymoon, Ellen returns to the Arden home and reacquaints herself with her two children. On learning about the marriage, she rushes to the hotel where the newlyweds are staying. As soon as Nick spots her, he panics and makes an excuse to convince Bianca that they should return home. Ellen, however, manages to get back before them and installs herself in the house by pretending to be a Swedish maid. She then encourages Nick to tell Bianca that his first wife is alive and well, but her problems are compounded when Nick learns that, far from being alone on the island, Ellen was stranded there with a male survivor. Ellen claims that the man was the bookish type, more interested in studying the island's geological features than her body. She duly attempts to pass off a weedy shoe clerk as her platonic island companion, but Nick has already discovered the mystery male to be handsome Steven Burkette. After initially pretending to go along with Ellen's story, Nick embarrasses her by revealing that he knows the truth. He also confesses everything to Bianca, who starts consulting analyst Dr. Schlick as a result. During the ensuing mayhem, Nick is arrested for bigamy. In court, the judge pronounces Ellen officially alive and Nick's marriage to Bianca null and void. This clears the way for a happy Arden family reunion, while Bianca winds up with Dr. Schlick.

BEHIND THE SCENES

Famous as the film that Marilyn Monroe never lived to complete, *Something's Got to Give* stands today not only as a prime example of a wayward star undermining the crumbling Hollywood studio system but also as a tantalizing reminder of what might have been had she not been fired in midproduction.

Lobby card for the documentary Marilyn, *which featured several minutes of footage from* Give.

Ellen (MM) tearfully returns home after being stranded on a desert island for five years.

The negative for most of the footage had supposedly been stolen or destroyed shortly after Marilyn died, but in 1982 eight boxes containing nearly six hours of raw footage were found in storage. Gaps in this material are probably the result of the removal of the best takes, which were edited together into a 35-minute version of the movie to help director George Cukor monitor progress during production. The location of this work-in-progress is unknown, but what remains contradicts the oft-repeated assertion by studio executives that Marilyn's acting, hampered by drugs, had the on-screen effect of being "in a kind of slow motion that was hypnotic." Indeed, if there is anything "hypnotic" about Marilyn's performance, it is the considerable tenderness and vulnerability that she was able to convey, together with her remarkably good appearance, at this troubled time in her life.

Looking superb in costume tests on April 10, 1962. The next morning, Marilyn was discovered in a barbiturate coma.

Intended as a remake of RKO's 1940 screwball comedy entitled *My Favorite Wife*, which had starred Irene Dunne and Cary Grant, *Something's Got to Give* was remolded into that subgenre known as the bedroom farce, which was quite prominent during the 1960s. In this type of comedy, glamorous characters in glamorous settings experienced difficulties of an amorous nature, usually revolving around—but never exploiting—bedroom high jinks. It would have been fascinating to see Marilyn Monroe bring her particular brand of overt sexuality to the bedroom farce, as opposed to the wholesome innocence of Doris Day, who became associated with the bedroom farce during this era. Interestingly, soon after *Give* had been shelved, the script was reworked by Fox into *Move Over Darling*, which was produced and released in 1963 as a Doris Day vehicle. Costarring the affable James Garner, *Move Over Darling* featured an altogether different cast and crew.

Marilyn and the studio began experiencing severe problems before the production of *Something's Got to Give* even began. Twentieth Century-Fox was teetering on the verge of bankruptcy, courtesy of the gargantuan production of *Cleopatra* that had been filming in London and Rome for two years. The historical epic was originally budgeted at around $5 million, but costs soon spiralled out of control. Sources vary as to what the final cost of the film was, but some speculate that it was close to $44 million while others estimate $37 million. The studio had been forced to sell part of the backlot and veto any new projects.

The only new production that was approved was *Something's Got to Give*, because its total budget was a mere $1 million, the same amount that Liz Taylor was commanding for appearing in—and often being absent from—the title role of Cleopatra. Marilyn was entitled to $100,000 for each of the two films that she still owed Fox under the terms of her 1955 contract. Although her recent movies had not been too successful, the studio executives were banking on her name to still be a sufficient enough draw at the box office to provide them with some much-needed funds.

Having shed 15 pounds, Marilyn appeared in excellent shape when she appeared in some costume and makeup tests on Tuesday, April 10, 1962, but the following morning, producer Henry T. Weinstein came face to face with her instability when he discovered Marilyn in a barbiturate coma at her newly purchased Brentwood home. He suggested abandoning the picture, but his superiors disagreed.

Once filming began on April 16, these decision-makers must have had second thoughts, for Marilyn, suffering from sinusitis and a virus, did not show up on the set for the first two weeks. Her first day of work was Monday, April 30, when, in spite of having a sore throat and a temperature of 101 degrees, she proved herself well prepared for the homecoming scene in which Ellen Arden encounters her children by the family swimming pool. The next day, Marilyn's virus flared up again, and she went home 30 minutes after arriving at the studio. On another occasion, she had to quit after almost fainting under a hair dryer. By May 10, she had turned up for only three of the first 18 shooting days and had actually worked on only one of those days.

Director Cukor (on whose real-life home the Arden house was based) had shot around Marilyn as much as possible, but now he was forced to shut down the set. Adding to the scheduling problem was a second major source of contention for Cukor, which involved the movie's script. Cukor

MM pretends to be a Swedish maid in a scene with Dean Martin and Cyd Charisse.

Ellen (MM) is reacquainted with her son (Robert Christopher Morley).

MM's last scene ever, opposite Wally Cox, on her 36th birthday.

had rejected the original script before production began, resulting in Walter Bernstein being commissioned to rewrite Nunnally Johnson's screenplay. No final version was ever officially approved, and Marilyn—who had voiced her own objections to the script—struggled with frequent changes and newly amended lines amid her nightly bouts of insomnia.

Nevertheless, she completed three days of work on May 14 through May 16, though one of those days was taken up entirely by the filming of a 15-second sequence with a reluctant dog. On May 17, production again ground to a halt when a helicopter carrying Peter Lawford landed on the Fox lot before noon and spirited Marilyn away to Madison Square Garden in New York, where she was to sing at the famous birthday bash for President John F. Kennedy. Permission had initially been granted for her departure, but in light of how far the movie was behind schedule, it had been withdrawn. Fox executives, as well as the cast and crew, were furious. Producer Weinstein, who at the time was also angry with Marilyn, later expressed regret that the studio had not swallowed its pride and turned the MM-JFK event to its own advantage by using it to promote *Something's Got to Give*.

To make matters worse, when she returned to work on Monday, May 21, Marilyn was suffering from exhaustion because of her trip and could not shoot any close-ups. The next day, Dean Martin showed up with a cold and, despite assurances from studio doctors that it was not contagious, Marilyn refused to work with him. Instead she went home and stayed there until Friday.

Right and above: *Marilyn took the set photographers totally by surprise when she emerged naked from the pool.*

At this tenuous juncture, Marilyn's insecurities began to heighten: She insisted that a blonde extra be removed because her hair color clashed with her own; and, after insisting that Cyd Charisse was padding her breasts, she threatened to do the same, necessitating alterations to all her costumes. When Marilyn did report to the studio, she was witnessed throwing up by the studio gates because of nerves. She remained in her dressing room for hours on end in order to avoid the dreaded cameras. Not even her team of three doctors—an eye/nose specialist, an internist, and an analyst—seemed able to help her.

Marilyn did enjoy a good day on Friday, May 25, during the shooting of the now-famous nude-swimming scene. She was supposed to swim in the pool in a flesh-colored bikini to simulate nudity, but when a cameraman complained that it was visible through the lens, Marilyn happily discarded the costume and frolicked naked in and out of the water. The still photographers present on the set that day could hardly believe their eyes or their luck. Marilyn agreed to allow these shots to be published in exchange for a slide projector and the promise that the photos would replace those of Elizabeth Taylor pasted around the world! Within a short time, images of the discreetly nude Marilyn appeared on magazine covers in 32 countries.

She turned up for work again the next day, but the four hours spent in the pool had aggravated her virus. Another prolonged period of absence followed before Marilyn reported back to the studio on June 1, her 36th birthday and, as events turned out, her last appearance in front of the movie cameras. This involved Ellen's attempt to pass off a weedy shoe clerk as her former island companion. Cukor, desperate to get some work done, refused to allow a birthday party to take place on the set until the end of shooting. Then, when the time did arrive, there were false pleasantries and a stilted atmosphere. "There was a pall over it," confirmed Weinstein. "We had gone through so much."

After the party, Marilyn made her final public appearance at a muscular dystrophy benefit at L.A.'s Dodger Stadium, where she was invited to throw out the first ball. Yet, the following week, she once again failed to

Following her swim, Marilyn hoped they would "give me some good nude lines to go with it."

Forced celebrations on the set, as Marilyn feeds director George Cukor some of her birthday cake at the end of her last working day.

A clear-eyed, youthfully pretty Marilyn in this costume test belies the studio's stories of her incoherent performance.

*Fade-out:
Goodbye, Norma Jeane . . . .*

show up for work this time because of "flared sinuses" and a temperature of 102 degrees. By now, however, few believed her excuses for missing work. The production was 16 days behind schedule and $1 million over budget, and Executive Vice-President Peter Levathes raged, "The star system has got way out of hand. We've let the inmates run the asylum and they've practically destroyed it."

On June 7, Marilyn allegedly visited a plastic surgeon after she slipped in the shower because of the "medication" she had taken and bruised her face. Fox responded by immediately contacting Kim Novak "and every other actress in and out of town," to replace her in *Something's Got to Give*. Meanwhile, Marilyn's psychiatrist, Dr. Ralph Greenson, interrupted his Swiss vacation to fly back to the States and guarantee studio executives that his patient would be fit and ready to work on the following Monday.

When Marilyn failed to show up for work the next day, Peter Levathes fired her and had his company file a $500,000 breach of contract suit. During 35 days of shooting, Marilyn had appeared at the studio on 12 days and had worked fully on only eight of these occasions. Soon after, Lee Remick was hired as Marilyn's replacement, only to be rejected by Marilyn's loyal friend, Dean Martin, who had costar approval. Fox was $2 million out of pocket with nowhere to go, and, although producer Weinstein had originally asserted that Marilyn "completely flouted professional discipline and is responsible for putting 104 crew members out of work," he later admitted, "She had enormous problems. It came with the territory, and the studio was naive to think that this wouldn't happen. I mean, if the picture was budgeted for an eight-week shoot, they should have budgeted it for a sixteen-week shoot, because they wanted a film with Marilyn Monroe."

Weinstein was not alone in his change of attitude. For the second time in her career, Twentieth Century-Fox caved in to Marilyn Monroe and reinstated her at twice her original salary. Sadly, however, Marilyn Monroe died on August 4, 1962—a month before the film was scheduled to resume production.